Philip Teasdale has written a bri  experience as an adoptive father account deserves to be read, help and hurt a parent can experience t traumatised child's difficulties. I attempts to explain, how fragn ~~~ome defensive in response to these difficulties. Philip's compassion for his daughter shines throughout.

Understanding adoptive parents' experiences, especially when the outcome is not what anyone would hope for, is such an important part of developing effective adoptive support and intervention. It is time we all gave up the 'happy ever after' myth of adoption and worked together to discover how to help the parents when we, as a society, ask them to do something extraordinary.

Kim Golding, consultant clinical psychologist and author

From the off, this is an open and honest, real-life account of what could be described as the story of the majority of adoptive families. Seeing it written down reminded me so much of that early time when I too thought I could mend all my own children's trauma.

Scott Casson-Rennie, adoptive dad and Head of Engagement & Delivery, Adoption UK

Inside Adoption is a brave, tragic and endearing account of an adoptive parent's experience of adopting a developmentally traumatised child, his experience of being a parent and his shift from naiveté and idealism to the harsher realities of not only how his child behaves towards him but how professionals behave towards him too… Prospective adoptive parents will get a salutary insight into the highs and lows of being a parent. Many adoptive parents will have their experience validated. Professionals working in the field will be challenged to review their perception of adoption by this account from a parent's perspective. All round, a very thought-provoking book.

Alan Burnell, co-founder and co-director of Family Futures

INSIDE
ADOPTION

A PARENT'S STORY

by Philip Teasdale

First published 2018

PCCS Books Ltd
Wyastone Business Park
Wyastone Leys
Monmouth
NP25 3SR
UK

Tel +44 (0)1600 891509
contact@pccs-books.co.uk
www.pccs-books.co.uk

Inside Adoption: a parent's story

British Library Cataloguing in Publication Data.
A catalogue record for this book is available from the British Library

ISBN 978 1 910919 37 8

Cover design by Jason Anscomb
Printed in the UK by Clays

Dedication

This book is dedicated to my family

Contents

Disclaimer

This book has been written under the pseudonym Philip Teasdale and is a true account of my thoughts, feelings and experiences as an adoptive parent. It also draws on my personal and work experiences as a therapist, adoption worker and adopter. The examples and cameos I have used are based on composites of those experiences; none of them are true representations of any individual and all the names and identifying information have been changed. Any similarities to real persons, alive or dead, are purely coincidental.

Acknowledgements

Many people have been involved in the production of this book and not even known it, and I would like to thank the extended family members, friends and neighbours who supported us as a family through many difficult years. I am also immensely grateful to our therapy team, whose dedication, empathic understanding and support has not only helped our daughter but also helped us to feel valued as adoptive parents and to stay, relatively, sane.

As a novice author, I knew little of preparing a manuscript or even if I could produce anything worth reading. My sincere thanks go to Jill, my test reader, who ploughed through all the chapters of this book in its original form, and Catherine, my editor. They provided much needed encouragement and advice, which has enabled me to tell my story in the way that I wanted to.

Finally, I would like to acknowledge and thank my wife, Anne, for her patience and unswerving support. Not only has she added her invaluable insight to this work but she has also put up with countless evenings and weekends while I sat at my computer and she provided endless cups of tea. She is a precious part of my life and of who I am, and our experience of adoption has shaped the both of us.

Preface

In October 2015, during National Adoption Week, a well-known newspaper printed a picture of some young children on its front page and asked its readers to consider being their 'forever family'. The next day, adoption support helplines were flooded with calls from willing volunteers.

The vast majority of these calls were from people with no previous desire to adopt and with no real knowledge or understanding of the adoption process. It showed just what an emotive subject this is. Seeing a child in acute need clearly evokes strong feelings.

To me, this seemed a reassuring response, however naïve it may have been. However, as those callers would have found out, adoption is a far from easy, straightforward process; it certainly isn't for everyone. There are good reasons why this is the case.

Adoption has changed hugely in the past few decades. Most of the children placed with adopters are no longer babies; by the time they meet their new parents they mostly have been exposed to a range of traumatic experience, both within their birth families and within the care system. Abuse in early childhood can have a significant impact that endures throughout the whole of the child's life, regardless of the care they receive in their adoptive homes. This poses very real challenges for those of us stepping into the role of adoptive parent.

Research has shown that the developmental stages from gestation up until two years of age are critical; during this period all children are susceptible to lasting damage from trauma of any type. In recent years there has been a wealth of publications regarding the effect of trauma on young minds and how it changes the psychology and neurobiology of those who are unfortunate enough to be exposed to it. This work has helped to change the way we think about children who have suffered at the hands of the people who were supposed to be caring for them. It has helped us understand their sometimes bizarre and frightening behaviours. It has changed the way we think about the care and help they subsequently need, and has informed new and better ways to parent them.

Sadly, like most advances in health and social care, it's taking a long time for this learning to become widely accepted and understood. Like rain that falls over high ground, it touches and revitalises those of us who have been painstakingly trudging up the mountain together but then it disappears into the rocks; it takes some time to seep into water courses and channels before finally ending up in the river. Eventually and very slowly, we will all get to taste this new understanding and know it to be true.

As the adoptive dad of an extremely traumatised and challenging young person, I can't wait for the day when this knowledge has been absorbed into the psyche of all caring professionals. Until then, I will continue, repeatedly and often painfully, to make my case to anyone with anything to do with adoption, and especially those in a position to make a difference. This book is a part of that process.

Much has been written about adoption, from all kinds of angles: from the new research and case study-based perspectives that shed new light on childhood trauma through to books on the adoption process and legislation, managing difficult behaviour and the adoption journey. Many of these have been written by professionals to explain various aspects of adoption from the outside looking in, and are mainly focused on the child, his or her needs and how those needs can be met. Many others have been written by adopters who have found success and fulfilment in the challenges of their adoptive parenthood.

Although this book is intended to add to that collection, its focus is not on the child; its focus is on the experiences and needs of the adopter.

First and foremost, adoption is a relationship, and therefore it is not a totally one-sided affair. Adoption is not just about the child. You can't have an adoption with just a child; it requires an adoptee *and* an adopter. Fortunately, in our case there were two of us sharing this adopter experience and, together, my wife and I set about trying to build the lifelong relationships that are unique to family life. We all counted equally in this endeavour, and we all needed certain things from it. This mutuality is in the very nature of relationship.

Having said that, you will discover as you read this book that it is primarily about me – about my thoughts, my feelings, my needs and even my trauma, as an adoptive parent. My wife, Anne, would have her own, unique account of this experience, as would my adopted daughter and my son. They are not my stories to tell.

This may sound self-indulgent, and even narcissistic, but the adopter's perspective on the impact adoption has had on them is remarkably under-represented in the literature. I believe this perspective is essential when trying to grasp an understanding of adoption from the inside out.

What is it really like to be the adoptive parent of a very traumatised child? Regardless of their reasons and motivation for adopting in the first place, most adopters simply want to be a 'forever mummy or daddy', just as the newspaper advert implied. Some end up with happy stories in which all those dreams come true. For many others, things are not so rosy. In the following pages, I will explain how it worked out for me and how my needs and aspirations were and were not met. I will explore and discuss the many relationships this led me into, in addition to the one I now have with my child. I will examine my own thoughts and feelings about adoption, with specific reference to my own experience; look at the evidence for adoption as it was presented then and how it is presented now, and examine its validity, and reflect on what the future may hold, as adoption continues to change to meet the changing needs of society.

Our adoption was difficult. Our daughter was, and remains, very troubled by her early experiences, and this, in turn, continues to affect our whole family. I suspect it always will. The things I have gained from adoption, I could never have predicted. The problems I have encountered would have made me run a mile, had I known about them up front. Had I been told that adoption could be like this I probably wouldn't have believed it; and here we are, like a third of adoptive families, struggling on... together... just.

A few years ago, I wrote an article about the difficulties of living with a violent child (Collins, 2015[1]). Many of the adopters who contacted me in response talked about their isolation and trauma, and the importance of having a voice. This book was written partly because we adopters don't have to, and nor should we, live our lives hidden away and in silence. Those of us who have not fared well and have had difficult and even dangerous children living with us still have an important place in society, and we should not be ignored. We are a significant part of the wider adoption story and we are not insignificant in number. For adoption to be understood in its fullest sense, then surely everyone who has a part in it needs to be included in any conversation we may have?

I hope this book speaks for the many of us for whom the joys of adoption have also brought a heap of problems, hard work and heartache. We deserve to be heard.

References

Collins D (2015). Living with your child's violence. *Therapy Today* 26(8): 22–26.

---

1. This article was written under a different pseudonym.

Chapter 1
Small beginnings

On our daughter's second birthday, I sat in front of my computer and wondered what she was doing. My fingers ran loosely over the keys.

There was something therapeutic about tapping my thoughts into words on a keyboard and seeing them reflected back at me from the screen. It was a kind of release, like thinking out loud and following those thoughts through to the feelings underneath. And you can say anything you like to a computer. It won't laugh, it won't sympathise and it won't hand back any well-meaning words of wisdom. I didn't know it then but writing down my thoughts and feelings was to become an ongoing part of my life.

I think it would have been easier if we had not already seen Jemma's photograph: blue eyes, rosy cheeks, bunches and all; a picture of hope and longing set in a blue cardboard frame. And now she was blowing out candles with someone else and doing who knows what.

When our son, Michael, was born, the same anticipation had been there, but it was different: it all just happened and I don't remember there ever being any time of pondering the future. We sort of fumbled our way through it. I remember odd parts of it, like driving across town to the hospital in the middle of the night, and I can vaguely recall the anxiety of the final 24 hours, the two cylinders of gas and air and the difficult delivery.

Even then, I just knew deep down things would be all right; but this time, waiting for the next addition to our family, there was a nagging uncertainty.

Being still and waiting for something to happen is not my strong suit. Give me something to do: a lawn to mow, a kettle to fix, a dog to walk, anything, only don't leave me just sitting here. Especially don't use those irritating words, 'Just try and push it to the back of your mind and get on with things' – the kind of words that all social workers use when they know you're in for a long wait.

Those mixed-up feelings had lasted several weeks. It seemed longer: a rollercoaster of emotion as Anne and I drifted in and out of euphoria and fear. The regular updates and reassuring phone calls from Caroline, our social worker, helped us to endure the constant delays, but we just hadn't anticipated that each week would feel like a year. Once all the paperwork was complete and the freeing order granted, we could move on to the next stage, but for now we just had to wait.

Eventually, in late June, three months after we were first told about her and a month after her birthday, we heard the news we were waiting for. We could actually meet Jemma face to face. It seemed strange and very daunting. After all this time, it was really going to happen. So, on a warm Thursday morning, armed with a pocketful of tissues, we pulled up in front of her foster home. Caroline was already sitting outside in her car, waiting for us.

I began shuffling about and tapping my right foot while we stood at the door, waiting for the bell to be answered. Anne nudged my arm and I stopped. The door opened and we were welcomed in by a short, bright-faced woman with a big smile – Julie.

The house was quiet. We sat down. Caroline introduced us to Julie, using Jemma's pet name for her, 'JuJu'. She probably sensed our tension and immediately went off to get Jemma, who was asleep in another room. We sat in silence, looking at each other.

After a couple of minutes, a small toddler, fitted with a dummy, silently dashed in, halted as if she had hit a brick wall, and briefly stood motionless, staring at us, before dashing back out again. Anne and I looked at one another, a little bit stunned. We didn't need words. I held out a tissue.

It was a funny feeling, sitting there, looking for the first time at our child-to-be. At that moment, we didn't even know that for sure. This toddler was possibly, probably, but not definitely, our daughter. It's a really strange situation to be in, rather like being slightly pregnant, except for the fact that obviously you can't be such a thing. Being a parent is an absolute: you either are or you are not. Under normal circumstances there is no maybe.

Julie returned to the room carrying Jemma, whose face was firmly embedded in Julie's neck. She prised Jemma from her stranglehold and tried, unsuccessfully, to sit her on her lap. Jemma eventually let go and buried herself in Julie's midriff instead. We sat and waited. Jemma stayed put. The four of us started to chat in slightly hushed tones, pretending to ignore Jemma and at the same time trick her into thinking that our visit was no big deal.

Looking back, what a pointless exercise our pretending was. Jemma only spoke about 20 words anyway, and most of them were just noises. She didn't need language to work out what was going on. We were scary strangers and that was all that mattered.

After about 15 minutes she relaxed a little, and at one point looked at me. It wasn't for long, just a second or two, but enough for her to check me out. She then burrowed back into JuJu.

And so we sat politely, having a fairly meaningless conversation for about half an hour. Jemma stayed glued to Julie's lap and our eyes stayed glued on Jemma. The room sat heavy with expectation.

When Julie got up to show us out, Jemma resumed the spider-monkey position. We said goodbye and lightly touched her on the arm. Outside, the sun was still shining.

Having to decide if I wanted this child to be my daughter was one of the oddest decisions of my life. There is nothing else I can compare it to. At this point we had no connection, no bond, no history, no relationship, and yet here we were, deciding if we wanted to spend the rest of our lives together. I had so many thoughts and feelings, and an underlying appreciation of the enormity of what it meant for all of us.

We were allowed one more visit and then we had to make that all-important decision: was this right for us? Did we want to be Jemma's forever mummy and daddy? At this stage it probably wasn't going to make any difference, but we went ahead anyway with the second visit. This time we were allowed to take Michael to meet his possibly, probably but not definitely new sister.

Michael had his reservations about being a brother, but one of his requirements had at least been met, in that Jemma was six years younger than him. He had made it clear that under no circumstances did he want an older, bossy sister. Otherwise, he was unsure about the whole thing, despite the selling job we had done on him. Having had us all to himself for more than eight years, it was bound to be a hard transition. From the outside it may have looked tough on him, but when it came down to it, we weren't actually adopting just so he would have a sibling. Even though that did feature in our thinking, ultimately we were adopting for us. We had suffered three miscarriages, and we had decided this would be the way we would complete our longed-for family.

That second visit confirmed in our minds and hearts that Jemma was for us, and even Michael seemed to take a shine to her and to his new position as the big brother in the family. Within weeks, the adoption-matching panel agreed the match and so it began: adoptive parenthood. From that moment onwards, life was never to be the same again.

In late summer Jemma began to arrive. Her transition from foster care to living with us was planned to take place in stages, over about two weeks. We were to move gradually from visiting her at the foster carers to taking her out for increasing periods of time during the day, to having her stay with us overnight. It was all set out in what was called an Introductions Plan. A suitable timescale for this process was originally mentioned in a book by the social worker Vera Fahlberg (1994) as part of a case study; I don't believe she ever intended it to be a one-size-fits-all measure but it had somehow become written into social work folklore. We had been warned not to get anything ready before we knew for certain we had been matched with Jemma and that she was going to be placed with us but the latter stages happened so fast that we were left with lots to do in a very short space of time. It was panic stations.

While Anne's father finished off the paintwork in the bedroom, we went shopping for all the equipment most young families acquire over nine months. We were looking lost and bewildered in one large store when we were approached by a helpful young woman, who was probably to regret doing so.

'Can I help?' she asked.

Buying a duvet sounds simple enough but it can get quite bewildering if you have no idea of the answers to questions about allergies and whether the child tends to get hot in the night. Then we came to the car seat and the sales assistant uttered the clincher: 'And how much does the child weigh?'

We had bluffed our way through until then but at this point we decided to come clean: we didn't have a clue. This was the first time we had told anyone, outside of family and close friends, that we were adopters. It was a strangely pleasant feeling.

The Introductions Plan fell apart almost immediately because the foster carers, having agreed to it only days beforehand, then decided they didn't want to go along with certain parts of it. This didn't worry us too much because we had already decided there were things about the foster placement that concerned us and we wanted to move Jemma in with us as quickly as we could. In the end, we jumped several steps of the plan and by early August she was with us. We were ready. We were more than ready – or so we thought.

The day Jemma finally and officially moved in was a Wednesday. I remember standing, holding her, and looking out of our bay window, showing her the world from her new home and, of course, showing her off to the world. Our neighbour came out to do some gardening and she looked up, pointed towards Jemma and gave a questioning nod of her head. I nodded back and she gave a broad smile. It felt good.

Anne and I were exhausted and relieved. Introductions are emotionally and physically draining for everyone. By the time you get to the end point you all need a holiday, just at the time the real work begins.

Regardless of how well we thought we had prepared, there were many things that surprised us and caught us out. For instance, we had not anticipated the amount of stuff that would come with Jemma. Yes, we had expected enough clothes and toys to part-fill a small bedroom but there were six large bags, or more. Then the big plastic tricycle with yellow wheels arrived, and the Cosy Coupe car and a host of other large toys. It seemed important, in those early stages, that she should have as many of her recognisable belongings around her as possible, and so we kept all these things indoors. This meant constantly having to be careful not to trip over anything and watching TV through the windows of the Cosy Coupe in the lounge.

From early on, we began to notice Jemma's odd behaviour. We had expected that the first few days would be fraught and difficult, and perhaps this prevented us from seeing the full relevance of some of the pandemonium that ensued.

She screamed the place down when we tried to get her to bed, and any sight of running water in the bathroom sent her into hysterics. When we gave her a banana cut into pieces she rammed the whole thing into her mouth, using both hands, until she could no longer chew because her mouth was so full. Anne ended up having to rake some of it out with her finger to prevent her choking. After that, we gave it to her a few pieces at a time. On our second or third evening together, we were busy dishing up our evening meal when we noticed that she was already sitting in her high chair, ready and waiting.

'Did you put her in there?' I asked Anne.

'No, didn't you?'

Seemingly, Jemma had scaled the high chair on her own and, ironically, put on her own safety harness. It turned out she was just as competent at getting into the car and buckling herself into her car seat. When it came to the meal itself, she could use a knife and fork beautifully, which was totally at odds with her immaturity and delayed development in many other areas.

She displayed a great deal of repetitive behaviour: rushing from room to room to complete some minor task like putting her socks on, only to return immediately to the original spot to take them off again. This usually culminated in the most disturbing behaviour of all: temper tantrums that lasted, literally, hours. These were accompanied by highly distressed screaming and frequent aggression, which was mostly directed at Anne, whose legs soon became covered in pinch marks, bites and scratches. There seemed little we could do to pacify her or quell these outbursts. We tried holding her, ignoring her, rocking her, distracting her; nothing worked, although we soon learned that she used the Cosy Coupe as a refuge when she was distressed and so we started to direct her towards it if we sensed a meltdown was on the way. It stayed in our lounge, obscuring the TV, for several months.

Jemma also brought with her a doll called Sophie. She stuck to Sophie like glue; the doll was so precious that we quickly found a Sophie replica that we kept in a cupboard in case the real Sophie was ever lost. Sophie had provided Jemma with comfort during long periods when she had been left alone, locked in her bedroom, and probably very fearful. This had obviously made a significant impact on her because it took some weeks and a great deal of coaxing before she would dare to venture out of her bed in the morning when she woke up, as most two-and-a-half-year-olds would do. She would just sit in bed, quietly and passively waiting for attention.

We began to deal with some of the issues piece by piece and as best we could. As it's not normal for children of that age to be so independent, we tried to make sure we did some things for her that she could do already herself. We made a great play of putting her shoes and coat on for her, helping her into and out of her high chair, and we took away the cutlery and gave her a plate of beans to get messy with. We helped her whenever she would let us. Eventually, we desensitised her to bathrooms and water by playing a very noisy, bubble bath-filled game in which we all got very wet. Michael really got stuck into this, and we almost flooded the house, but it was worth it.

As those first weeks ticked by, we saw a change in Jemma and, as our social worker had predicted, things soon began to settle down... a little. However, the tantrums and frantic, repetitive behaviour persisted and, if anything, got worse. Or perhaps we just became more affected by them and by our apparent inability to sooth her and sort the problems out. I guess that was on both our minds: that we had to fix things in some way so we could start functioning as a normal family, or as near to that as we could.

But then, is an adoptive family ever a 'normal' family? The impact of abuse in the early life of a child is often very significant and can result in severe problems that adopters ultimately have to deal with. All prospective adopters know this and, like us, expect to be able to deal with it.

I remember struggling with some of the questions during our assessment. At that stage, almost everything we talked about was in the abstract. That is to say, we had no experience of adoption, what it would be like, or how we would feel, but we still had to give answers that we could justify on how we would react in certain situations. What if a child smeared poo up the walls? What then? What if they hid under the table all day, stored food in their bedroom or repeatedly bit the cat? How would we deal with that? What would really test and press our red buttons? What were our red buttons? Michael had never done anything really untoward, so our buttons had generally remained unpressed. His terrible-twos lasted for about one day, and on the odd occasion he got out of hand, a lightly raised voice brought him back down to earth. He was a bright, co-operative, well-behaved little boy, who had brought nothing but joy into our lives. We hadn't experienced any of the problems we were expected now to consider.

Although we had listened to all the advice, we were unprepared for many of the real-life consequences of adoptive parenthood. Jemma had been with us for just a few months when, on a trip to our nearby shops, she lay down on the pavement, screaming, kicking her heels and rolling around, while Anne tried to get her to her feet and calm her down. An elderly lady stopped to make some unhelpful comment to Jemma, which was clearly aimed at Anne. At that point, Jemma obligingly got up and kicked the old lady on the shin. Anne apologised, even though there was some divine justice in the action. We soon learned you need broad shoulders as an adoptive parent.

The 'Form F' we had completed during assessment actually referred to us as applying to be 'prospective substitute parents'. I found this an insulting term. I didn't want to be a substitute dad, and I didn't see myself as offering a substitute home and a substitute family. If I was going to do this, it was not to be a stand-in for the 'real thing'; it was to have a child I would acknowledge, raise and love as my own. I wanted to be a real dad. As it turned out, I wanted to be Jemma's dad.

Now, many years later, I wonder if, from the perspective of some adopted children at least, substitute is an appropriate term after all, however hard that may be for an adopter to contemplate. Nancy Verrier's book *The Primal Wound* (1993) sheds light on the lives of adoptees and the experience of being separated from one's birth family. It explores the pain, trauma and loss this causes and how it can affect adopted children for life. No matter how caring, able and dedicated their adoptive parents and siblings are, for some children, they can never replace or replicate their birth family. Their adoptive family will always be a substitute, regardless of how much they feel loved and a part of it.

I also found that things were different for me, as a parent, with my adopted child, and I see now that this was bound to be reflected in my relationship with Jemma, no matter how deep and meaningful that relationship became. Having a child by birth and an adopted child meant we were often asked about those issues of difference and how we felt about it. This curiosity wasn't helpful: we were simply trying to be a normal family and the questions highlighted the fact that adoption is not a natural process; it's an attempt to replicate something that is natural. I used to duck the issue, saying that I felt the same towards them both in some ways and not in others, in the same way that any parent will feel different towards their different birth children.

This was probably true at the time, and I believe it reflected the hope and dreams I had started out with.

However, for me, there is a clear difference. Putting it into words is less clear. I do love them both and very differently. We have unique relationships and my whole experience as an adopter has been dramatically different to my experience as a birth parent. Initially, perhaps, I held the sentiment that I should be able to love any child equally and this would be the right thing to do as a parent, but I let go of those ideas a long time ago and, as you will see later in this book, my experiences have forced me to examine myself on a more emotional plane and have changed my perceptions.

I don't believe in love at first sight and I can't tell when I first began to love Jemma. The relationship between children and their parents carries so much with it, and with birth children the bonds that tie us to our offspring begin even before they are born. For me and Michael, this was a natural process that required little effort on my part. In adoption, this opportunity does not exist. In those very early days of caring for Jemma, I think I was attracted by her sheer energy and resilience. It was as if you could mow her down with a steam roller and she would just pop back up again, like a cartoon character, and as she took to men rather than women, I got all the good stuff. I usually received all the attention and the hugs when I arrived home and she was always ready to play any game, even though her interest didn't usually last long. I slowly bonded with her and hoped she was attaching to me, and as time went on we formed a closeness; I came to feel that we belonged to one another.

For Anne, things took much longer. Being assaulted on a daily basis takes its toll on you, even if the perpetrator is less than two feet tall. Some days when I got in from work she had been through a horrid time. I would just step in with Jemma's care and leave Anne to sort herself out and manage any emotional damage on her own, in the space this provided. In retrospect, I think that I could have been far more supportive of Anne in those early stages. The challenges she faced as Jemma's new mum probably played into some of the insecurities I know she carried from childhood, but there never seemed time to speak or even think about this aspect of parenthood. Most of our thoughts, conversation and focus were on Jemma and everything else came a poor second. Thankfully, Anne is a really good mum who had worked with children in a range of challenging situations during her career. She was the one making sense of all the odd behaviour and coming up with ways to help Jemma work through it. I was learning from her as I went along. We tried to keep Michael on an even keel and give him enough space and attention too, but given his laid-back nature, he seemed to adapt to the new dynamic and just got on with life. Building bonds of affection with our new daughter, under those circumstances, was highly demanding.

Before Jemma was placed with us, I was living in that abstract dream world of pre-adoption, where hope and optimism reign as the willing partners of denial. I believed that, even though there would be problems to deal with along the way, things would come out well in the end. After all, we were good, resourceful and intelligent people, and we had a track record as the parents of one delightful, well-adjusted and bright nine-year-old. What could possibly go wrong?

In the small, cosy bedroom that we had created for Jemma in her new home was a child's wardrobe, on one door of which was a long mirror. After the first few months, we covered it with pictures of baby animals because we noticed she would sit in bed and stare at her own reflection for several minutes on end in a very distracted and disturbing way. We instinctively knew this behaviour was odd, but we didn't fully appreciate its relevance. Over time, it was to become very clear.

References

Fahlberg V (1994). *A Child's Journey Through Placement*. London: BAAF.

Verrier NN (1993). *The Primal Wound*. Baltimore: Gateway Press.

Chapter 2
When love is not enough

The tide was nearly in when we counted our way down the six stone steps onto the beach. We had eaten early to avoid the crowds and now, while they were off in search of their tea, we had the small strip of beach all to ourselves. We stood there for some time, watching the waves slide towards us and disappear into the sand with a hushed whisper. One ran up and tried to touch our toes and we jumped back, Jemma squealing with glee; then another, and another, and for the next 20 minutes this became a great game as, with each advancing wave, we waited until the last possible moment before reeling backwards up the beach with shrieks of laughter. It was a rare moment, one of the few times that holiday when Jemma dared to come out from beneath her blanket of fear and distrust and showed us a glimpse of the little girl beneath – a lovely, friendly, fun-loving girl, momentarily at ease with herself and with us.

I think she was emotionally about six or seven that day, even though she had just celebrated her 13th birthday. We ended a very difficult week saying 'Never again!' – as we did every year.

Jemma's trauma runs deep within her. When she came to live with us she was only in her third year of life but she had already suffered more abuses and ordeals than, for most of us, would be imaginable in a lifetime. Included in this were five moves within the care system, some into circumstances that were equally unsafe and damaging as the ones she had been removed from. The damage this created has affected every part of her – her functioning, thoughts and emotions. It reveals itself in many ways and, although these have altered as she has grown up, the underlying nature of her distress has not.

At the time we adopted her there was still a big debate going on about what counted most, nature or nurture. This was in part an attempt to answer the difficult question of whether we are shaped by our genetics or our environment, and how much. Alongside this debate ran various ideas about how much the damage done to abused children in early childhood could be fixed or reversed, and the ultimate question, 'Is love enough?'

Different ideas were held by different people, who often did not hold back from sharing their views with us, even when they saw the problems we were having. They broadly fell into three camps: those who believed 'love changes everything'; those who believed that 'bad blood will out' regardless of what you do, and those who were unsure about the whole debate.

I remember getting quite hot under the collar when we were just about to meet Jemma for the first time and a friend tried to warn us about 'taking on a child you know nothing about'. These are his words, not mine. His concern was, I think, based on prejudice, and on some of the things he'd heard from other adopters. He may have meant well, but at the time it felt like a snipe at our ability to parent. While I didn't believe that love was enough on its own, I did believe we were good enough parents to achieve what the social workers had implied we needed to do in order to help repair some of the damage done to Jemma before we met her.

The big thing we believed we had in our favour was that Jemma was only two, giving us plenty of scope to help her recover from her past experiences and attach to us. The general assumption was that older children who are placed for adoption have generally been subjected to more abuse over a longer period of time than babies and toddlers, and so are likely to be more affected. Hence, having such a young child placed with us was potentially brilliant news.

We soon discovered that it didn't make things any easier. Jemma was constantly on the go and had many triggers, some of them quite subtle and impossible to predict with any certainty. They produced only one response – anger. This was made worse by her lack of language, so it could be hard to differentiate between the 'terrible twos' and the effects of her traumatic past. As time passed, the anger didn't and, despite our optimism, we were pretty much in the dark about what might be going on for her.

In the 1950s the psychoanalyst Donald Winnicott had introduced the idea of 'good-enough parenting' (Winnicott, 1965) and this made great sense, in combination with John Bowlby's attachment theory and his ideas about the 'internal working model' (Bowlby, 1969; Holmes, 1993). None of this had been mentioned to us during our preparation to adopt, and we knew nothing about it.

These theories were temporarily side-lined in the latter part of the 20th century. They had been unpopular with some feminists because Winnicott and Bowlby both stated that children primarily need their mothers; this was thought to place an unreasonable responsibility for parenting on women and meant the mother was blamed if the child turned out to be less than perfect. There was also little scientific evidence to back any of these models, as the neuroscience of trauma was in its infancy and the research methods that have since enabled rapid advances in this field had not been developed. Even the word 'trauma' was not widely used in the vocabulary of childhood maltreatment at that time. Trauma was something that happened to war veterans or survivors of serious accidents, not mistreated babies. Babies suffered abuse, deprivation and loss, and most of what we were told in our preparation classes was based on observational or even anecdotal information.

Thankfully, knowledge about the impact of our emotional and physical environment in childhood has grown considerably in recent years and continues to do so. The nature versus nurture debate is largely resolved, and it is now generally accepted that our genetics and our environment (epigenetics) both have important roles in shaping the people we become.

In addition, there is a much greater acknowledgement of the critical importance of the gestation period and a child's first two years of life, in terms of development. The lasting effects of trauma at this stage have been proven by numerous studies in neuroscience, supporting the hypotheses of Winnicott, Bowlby and others. At birth, our brains are not fully developed; they continue to grow – they approximately double in weight in the first year alone – along with all the wiring and connections that determine our unique configuration and personal operating systems. Many factors contribute to this growth, including our diet, environment and the care we receive. These all contribute to the formation of our individual neurobiological and psychological systems. We all need 'good-enough parenting' and loving contact with at least one attachment figure for this to go well and for our development to continue healthily.

In terms of development, this early period could be regarded as 'the time of our lives'. This is the phase when many of our characteristics are formed and set in place for life. It is the stage of development when the mix of biology and environment is at its most potent and, although we all continue to grow, change and be affected by new experiences, how we do that is influenced by that early definition of self. We make sense of new things by reference to what we have previously experienced.

The psychotherapist Carl Rogers talks about us each living in a perceptual field (Rogers, 1951), from which we define our reality. In other words, we each hold our own set of truths about ourselves and the world we live in, and these are primarily based on our experience. This does not seem dissimilar to the working models that Bowlby described, in which we define the world based on the way we personally experience it and we define our self by how we experience ourselves within the world.

We begin to develop these individual ways of being as soon as we are born and even before that we are affected physiologically in the womb by our maternal environment. In a way, we learn by what we experience and that knowledge is incorporated into our sense of who we are and what the world is like. Our experience becomes part of us.

Jemma had learned lots of things by the end of her first two years. She learned that when she needed changing it often didn't happen; when she was hungry she wasn't fed; when she was cold she was not given warmth. Worse than that, when she acted out her purely biological instinct to scream in order to have her needs met, it did not work. Rather than bringing comfort it brought nothing, and sometimes it even brought violence. She consequently deduced that adults could not be trusted and that she had no worth. She also learned to survive.

So, even though it was quite funny at the time, when we first gave her that cut-up banana and she crammed it all into her mouth with both hands, she wasn't simply doing an impression of a greedy hamster; she had learned the rule of 'Eat when you can', because you never know when food will be available again or who might steal it. That behaviour was an expression of her reality and an example of how she had made sense of her world up until that point.

Many of her behaviours were similarly disturbing and seemed to be linked to her past experiences. They were how she had adapted to her life and, even if that life no longer existed for her, these adaptations had got her this far and she was not going to simply let go of them. As she grew, her behaviours did too, although the motives behind them stayed pretty much the same.

This aspect of her life is one that has confused most of the people – friends and professionals alike – who have come to know us. Although trauma as a word, a concept and a reality is now freely applied to people of all ages who have been frightened and abused in a variety of terrible ways, it is still seen as something that can be somehow treated, if recognised. Early childhood trauma is indelible. It cannot be worked through, rubbed out, obscured or forgotten.

If I take a piece of paper, scrunch it up and throw it around the room all day, it will bear that damage forever. Yes, I can straighten it out, press it and make it more or less serviceable once again, but even if I write the most profound and poetic verse on it, I will still be able to see the scars of its previous ordeal. And if I try to put it through a printer with all the other sheets of paper, it will most likely jam and smear the ink. Working with this piece of paper will require more care, skill and effort than those pristine sheets that came straight out of the packet.

By the time Jemma moved in with us, she had been very scrunched up indeed. Regardless of her genetic make-up, she had been marked by all her bad experiences pre- and post-birth. This had not only defined her view of herself and the world; it had also shaped her physiologically.

My own early life had been very different to hers in just about every way. For me, home had always been safe, warm and welcoming: a place I felt valued and loved, and where there was an unspoken interplay between my parents in their care of me. Mum was the cautious worrier, Dad the calm, encouraging force that enabled me to take the everyday risks I needed in order to develop.

I can remember few childhood incidents that were really distressing. One of these was when I must have been about seven or eight and had the misfortune to move into Miss Barker's class. She was renowned for her stern approach. It was one dull afternoon and we were all engaged in drawing endless circles and adding numbers and hands to make clock faces showing the times she had chalked on the board. Bored, I began fiddling with the drawstring on the small bag of marbles in my pocket, and one dropped out and bounced noisily on the worn, wooden floor. She was out of her chair like a rocket, rushed over, grabbed me from my desk and, with one hand, raised the leg of my grey shorts, and slapped me with the other. It stung. More than that, it was embarrassing, especially when I began to cry. The other kids looked up, startled; some sniggered, and then they all got back to their circles, trying not to attract any attention to themselves.

I can't say that the incident marked me for life, even though the old bag confiscated the marbles and I never did get them back. But it seems significant because I can remember it now, whereas I don't specifically remember much else from that period. I know that, like most children, I also experienced other events more distressing than this and I believe I was able to assimilate this one and all the others because I had received good-enough parenting. This not only helped me to establish a good sense of who I am and how I fit into the world; it also meant I could withstand the shocks and frustrations that we all face in life. It made the marble incident stressful, but not life threatening, and even at that young age I was able to contextualise, process and move on from it. Jemma, on the other hand, had not been fortunate enough to have such a trouble-free existence and had not been able to develop a firm sense of self.

We had been told that she had delayed development, which seemed like a term that could be used to explain a host of problems and we didn't have the knowledge then to understand the significance of everything we were observing. Although we hadn't recognised it, Jemma's fragile sense of self was evident throughout those early months following her placement with us when she would sit in bed and stare at the little girl who appeared in her bedroom mirror. Her sense of self was so weak that she was unable to recognise her own reflection.

Her earliest experiences of privation and violence had led to this lack of personal identity, just as it had left her with a perception of the world as a dangerous place where adults cannot be trusted. These factors most likely resulted in her living in constant fear that something bad was going happen and even that she might be annihilated at any moment. I imagine that she was very, very frightened when she moved in with us, and that intense fear stayed with her for a considerable time. I find it hard to comprehend that anyone could experience continual fear in the absence of any real threat and in the company of loving care but, with what I know now, I realise this is probably how it was for Jemma.

It was implied that, with the right care, she would improve and could catch up on some missed milestones, although this couldn't be guaranteed. At first, we were largely content to put everything down to her disrupted past, trusting that things would settle down and begin to get better. I remember saying to our social worker that I couldn't wait until Jemma could talk so that we could explain things to her and get to the bottom of some of the difficult behaviour she was displaying. If only it had been that simple. That she was so young and had no language when all her abuse and neglect took place is very significant.

We all make sense of the world through language. Language enables us to symbolise events and feelings and record them in our memories for later reference. Significant events in our lives also get laid down as body, or somatic, memories. In other words, they are internalised as a feeling or a sensation linked to what happened. The brain's limbic system is the key component in the storage and retrieval of these emotional memories.

I noticed a counselling colleague take some paracetamol one day and asked if she was okay. She told me it was her son's birthday. He was now in his late teens but she said she always felt slightly unwell on his birthday, with stomach and body pains and a headache. She explained that his birth had been very traumatic and was a horrible experience. We got talking about trauma and somatic memory, which seemed to be at the root of her physical sensations. She said it helped to speak about it and later that day, either through our conversation or the paracetamol or both, told me she felt much better. Likewise, I also have found that, when I am experiencing difficult or unwanted thoughts and feelings, it helps me to dispel them if I can talk about them with a trusted friend, especially if they relate to something from the past and don't belong in the present. Having this autobiographical recall of life experiences helps us to understand what happened to us and how we feel about it. Expressing our feelings helps us to process them, which is particularly important when they are troubling and complex.

Traumatic body memories are often stored in a disorganised way and are difficult to manage or express. When an older child or adult is traumatised, they have a cognitive memory of what happened, alongside the emotional one stored in their limbic system. If the trauma takes place preverbally, before a child can talk, there is an added problem. Infantile amnesia occurs at approximately age three and is a well-known stage of development: the brain essentially reorganises its cognitive and memory functions. This does not mean that infants do not retain their early memories, it just means that they cannot recall them cognitively. As a result, they have no narrative with which to communicate or put them into context. Theodore Gaensbauer (2002) argues that therapists and parents have a crucial role in helping the traumatised child achieve verbal understanding of a preverbal traumatic event as this is essential in helping them make sense of their experience.

Imagine what it might be like if every time someone lightly touches your arm you turn around and punch them, or every time you smell a particular cologne you wet yourself and run away, but you have absolutely no idea why. How disturbing would that be?

Jemma had a number of terrifying preverbal memories that could be triggered by a smell, a sound, a touch or any number of other non-conscious reminders, causing bodily sensations that she didn't understand and could not put into context or explain. So, even when she did learn to talk, this did not help her, or us, get to the root of the problem. This was to cause all sorts of issues in later years, when we were trying to help her unravel some of the damage. She simply had no words for her distress, and so could not readily access it or express it. It had become stuck inside her brain and body as a trauma memory, or a set of feelings that she was living with but could not understand or verbalise. She had no way to express what she was feeling other than through her behaviour.

When she did begin to develop speech, she didn't seem to understand it or use it like most of us do. She rapidly acquired a large vocabulary but her comprehension lagged very much behind. This could be confusing for those around her because she could verbally construct long sentences using big words but she couldn't understand simple concepts like colour. This didn't worry us too much, as we appreciated that her learning would be delayed and our immediate concern was for her emotional wellbeing and behaviour, not her educational performance. It was an issue for the nursery staff, however, who were relentless in their pursuit of milestones, regardless of her rocky start in life. Their expectations created an extra pressure and made things worse.

My initial hope that things would become easier once we could converse with one another soon faded. The problem behaviours that I believed would go away, once we could talk about them, didn't, and it got worse as she got older; the gap between her level of functioning and that of other children her age grew wider and more noticeable. We began to consider her in terms of three ages: a chronological age, a cognitive age and an emotional age. Her cognitive age lagged some way behind her chronological age, and her emotional age varied, depending on the stress she was under at any moment. It could fluctuate quite dramatically within a day, from hour to hour, and even from minute to minute. She was in a continual state of anxiety about one thing or another and when she was under additional stress, her emotional age would plummet and she would have temper tantrums that lasted hours.

The fact that this could be down to her being scared never occurred to me. I put it down to 'the terrible twos', to her wanting her own way or wanting attention. It was not until Jemma was in her teens that she was able to express her fear in ways I could begin to understand. Even though she could not fully articulate what it was that frightened her, the fact that she was frightened was very clear from her presentation. She would become visibly alert and distressed yet, initially at least, contained. It took me some time to get my head around what she meant when she said, as she frequently did, that she felt unsafe.

Her definition of safety was different to mine and what most people would recognise. When she was fearful, it didn't necessarily mean that she thought she was going to be physically harmed in that moment, although this could also be in her mix of thoughts and feelings. Often it was about emotional safety, which was based on her trauma memories and internalised perception of the world as a bad and dangerous place full of adults who could not be trusted, who were always leaving her and who sometimes hurt her because she was a worthless person who deserved it. From that perspective, getting too close to someone, accepting that you are loved, enjoying the experience of being hugged or simply having meaningful eye contact was so far outside of what she knew the world really to be like that it was threatening. The 'good stuff', as most of us would see it, conflicted so much with her perception of the world and herself that it was frightening.

In his propositions about personality, Carl Rogers (1961) theorises that, when we experience something that is inconsistent with our self-concept, we experience it as a threat and defend ourselves against it. We resist change. We can only assimilate new experiences into our self-concept and so grow and change if we do not feel threatened. As Jemma felt unsafe in so many circumstances, this compromised her ability to adapt to her new life with us. Just as some abused people return repeatedly to abusive partners and situations because it's what they know, possibly Jemma felt safer being shouted at or hurt than accepting kind words or a cuddle. Only if she could be helped to change that view of life would she be able to function in the world as most of us do.

Early in my practice as a therapist, I saw a client who had been referred to me with repeated episodes of depression and anxiety. Marie had worked her way through most of the services our NHS trust offered over the preceding three years, gradually feeling more distressed and finding no resolution. When we first met in our department's reception area, I could see she was shaking. I reflected this to her and she acknowledged that it had taken all of her limited resources to come to see me.

The room I was allocated at that time was long and thin, with three low chairs and a small table at one end. When we entered it, I saw the look of panic on Marie's face. For a moment we just stood there. I asked her if she was okay, although clearly she was not. I could see that she was unlikely to be able to walk the 10 feet to the end of the room where the chairs were, so I took a chair from reception and placed it just inside the room. She sat down and asked if I would open the window, and we spent the better part of an hour saying very little, she perched on her orange plastic chair near the door and me at the other end of the room getting very cold. Over the next six sessions she gradually moved her chair down the room until we were both sitting together and we began, very slowly, to try and unpick what she was feeling.

In my work with traumatised people, I have often wondered if there is a seventh condition that precedes the six that Rogers describes as being necessary and sufficient for therapeutic change to occur.[1] The seventh condition I propose is that the client feels safe, or at least safe enough, to engage in a meaningful therapeutic relationship with the counsellor. Rogers does regard it as a requirement for fostering constructive creativity; he says that psychological safety and psychological freedom are essential for this. He considers these two conditions can be established by processes that closely resemble his central conditions, which hardly seems surprising (Rogers, 1961). Maslow's hierarchy of needs also posits safety as a fundamental precondition to meeting psychological needs such as belonging and being in relationship (Maslow, 1987).

In my role as a person-centred counsellor, the creation of a safe and containing space for my clients is arguably a natural consequence of how I work and it could be assumed, therefore, that safety is implicitly derived from putting the six necessary and sufficient conditions into practice. However, if this is the case, in some instances it would mean putting the cart before the horse because some of my clients are simply too apprehensive and anxious to fully engage in the process of therapy when we first meet and they need to settle in and feel safe before we can do anything constructive. At this stage, an assortment of fears can extinguish the spark of what could go on to be a meaningful

---

1. The six conditions are, briefly summarised, that the therapist and client are in 'psychological contact'; the client is in a state of 'incongruence' – that is, feeling vulnerable or anxious; the therapist is congruent or 'integrated in the relationship'; the therapist feels unconditional positive regard for the client; the therapist has an empathic understanding of the client's internal frame of reference, and the therapist is able to communicate this empathic understanding and unconditional positive regard to the client (Rogers, 1957).

relationship, and I think of safety as a stage of pre-therapy that some clients need to pass through. I have noticed this to be critical in so many situations that I now always make it a separate consideration, especially in the early stages of any new therapeutic relationship.

In my subsequent work with Marie, I discovered that, although she had tried to get help from different services, she had never managed to feel safe enough to really do any work on herself and her problems. Most of this provision had been time bounded and structured in a way that meant she could never quite get to that point of feeling safe enough.

Safety was not something Jemma had ever known. Unfortunately, she didn't, never has, and probably never will feel completely safe. One of the many things I didn't initially understand about her behaviour and our inability to change it was that, to assimilate her new experiences into her self-construct, she needed the absence of fear. This was a precondition for her to be able to move on from her views of the world as dangerous, other people as untrustworthy and herself as worthless. That is why I say that, even though her behaviour changed as she grew older, the motives behind it stayed the same: she was always rigidly protecting herself against the next assault on her being.

Accompanying her sense of fear was a very high level of anxiety that was easily provoked by a range of stressors. Stress for her was probably not the same as it is for most of us, because of her heightened sense of alarm. She had an extremely heightened sensitivity to even minor daily happenings and was in a state of constant hypervigilance. This is how she had adapted in order to survive her early life, but the downside was that now she could experience even small, everyday frustrations as major threats and intrusions into her world. She was mentally tuned to detect the slightest danger and be ready to respond to it at a second's notice, because that was what she believed she needed to do to stay alive.

This anxiety could be brought on by trivial things, like noticing that the petrol in the car was running low, or a fly in the house, or an open window. If Anne and I both happened to leave her alone in a room without warning, it could trigger a strong sense of abandonment; if one of us went shopping and returned home five minutes later than expected, she was convinced we had died in a horrific car crash and she would break into a panic. She could catastrophise almost about anything.

When asked simple questions like, 'Which packet of sweets would you like?', she would also go into a meltdown, as this involved her making a decision and she knew she would make the wrong one, and then the world would surely end. Buying clothes was another trigger and required days of preparation and rehearsing before we dared risk emptying the changing rooms in Debenhams yet again.

All these simple tasks of daily living spelled danger to her, in one form or another; she was constantly scanning her horizons for anything that threatened her sense of safety. This was a direct result of her early life, when having a highly developed ability for observation and alertness had been important survival skills and her predictions of harm very probably were well founded. Consequently, every new situation was stressful for her, and whenever she became stressed, her emotional age would plummet and her behaviour would become that of a distressed and angry toddler. This continued beyond her eighth, ninth and 10th birthdays and into her teens.

On most Sunday afternoons, I would take Jemma to a nearby country park. This was to give Anne and Michael an hour or two of quiet, and Jemma was always better out of the house than in. Wide-open places with few people around suited her and allowed her space and freedom. We would walk and talk, play tag and, at some point, end up sitting on a bench eating ice creams. In these moments, with me alongside her in a fairly unruffled mood, she could feel calm enough to regulate her emotions and talk about the preceding week and the chaos that we had all been through. It made as little sense to her as it did to us. She was mostly confused by it; she knew roughly what had happened but had no memory of the specific details and was totally unable to recall what was going on for her during those crazy episodes of emotional overload.

This apparent loss of memory was not a convenient ploy. Any perceived threat or challenge to her psychological system caused a surge of stress hormones – adrenaline and cortisol – as her body prepared for fight, flight or freeze. This flood of chemicals to her brain produced acute arousal and she could not rationalise, verbally communicate or 'pull herself out of it' when it happened. She was so flooded with stress hormones that she literally could not think and became a toddler, exhibiting a toddler's behaviour and relying on the adults around her to contain her until she returned to a place where she could regulate her own emotions again. She could remember very little of these episodes because the event and what had caused it did not register anywhere in her conscious mind. The parts of the brain responsible for memory were effectively offline, and so she really didn't have any memory of them.

This kind of emotional dysregulation is common in children stuck in this stress-based cycle. Picking up the cues, anticipating them ahead of any major blowout and helping Jemma to maintain a stable emotional state were key to helping reduce her outbursts. The cues were not always obvious, despite their emotionally explosive consequences. We became used to watching out for signs and small changes in Jemma that signalled stress and steering her away from situations that were evidently causing her distress. We learned to understand her behaviour as a language in itself and long after she had developed good verbal skills we continued to understand what she was communicating through her actions as much as through her speech.

Some of her triggers were undoubtedly driven by an intense need to have control. This was another defence technique she had learned from living in a hostile environment where self-preservation was an imperative. She needed to be in control and self-reliant in order to feel safe. Any attempt to curtail this or take control away from her could make her feel threatened and she was likely to react with aggression. Simply trying, for instance, to get her to stop what she was doing and come to the table to eat could be enough, some days, to send her into a meltdown. As a toddler, her physical aggression manifested as tantrums, biting and scratching, but it grew in severity as she got older, into physical violence and threats, and she also became verbally aggressive and very manipulative. She excelled at splitting and creating chaotic situations where she was in control.

Like many adopted children, education posed serious challenges for Jemma. School was a perpetual cause of anxiety and a predictable stressor in terms of her behaviour. Her anxiety always increased and her behaviour deteriorated during term time, and especially in the days approaching the start of a new term. She was not equipped for the challenges of sitting still, getting along with her peer group and being taught.

We all use high-level cognitive functions, called executive skills, to meet challenges and achieve goals every day (Dawson & Guare, 2004). These are not only thinking skills but also skills of emotional regulation, thinking before you act and attention. Executive skills help us manage our feelings and monitor our thoughts as well as plan, organise and manage our time effectively. They also contribute to memory of the task in hand.

It is known that trauma during early childhood, when the brain is undergoing its most radical period of growth and development, can seriously affect brain function (Glaser, 2000), and this includes the development of these skills. Children who have been abused often do poorly at school and this cannot be simply explained on the basis of IQ alone (Lansdown, Burnell & Allen, 2007). To effectively undertake classroom learning requires a good degree of executive functioning. The ability to pay attention, to organise materials and new information and to remember what we have done previously is required. We also need cause-and-effect thinking to prevent us from repeating the same mistakes and the skills to develop new strategies.

It slowly became clear to us, even before we had heard the term, that Jemma's executive functioning was severely impaired. This was largely developmental and a consequence of her early years, but her constant state of fear made matters worse. When under stress, we all suffer a loss of executive functioning. If you have ever been unable to find your car keys just as you are about to leave for work, you have probably been a victim of this. You begin to panic, you can't concentrate and your mind goes blank. You don't remember where you put them and, in that moment, you can't even recall when you last had them. Stop! Breathe. Relax. The chances are, if you can overcome that feeling of panic, your executive skills will be able to function again, and you will remember that you wore your other jacket yesterday and your keys are in the pocket.

Similarly, my therapy clients often express a worry that they are losing their memory and struggling to complete everyday tasks: they missed Uncle Fred's birthday last week and went shopping for milk but returned with eggs and potatoes. This is most often a result of their executive skills being affected by underlying anxiety and depression and, sure enough, as their depression lifts, they find their executive functioning returns.

Jemma's stress-filled existence, in which she rarely felt completely safe and was always on high alert, meant that her poorly developed executive skills were further compromised. Her organisational skills were practically non-existent, she had a very patchy memory and she simply could not take in new concepts or ideas. It wasn't that she wouldn't do schoolwork; it was that she couldn't. Getting other people to understand this was very hard.

Paradoxically, as she grew older we noticed she had some special talents that were directly related to the way she functioned. For instance, she could spot a parking space a mile off in a crowded car park and if any household item was moved or removed from its usual place she noticed it instantly. She struggled to remember even very simple lists and tasks but could memorise whole passages from books we read to her or from her favourite films and recite them back to us at length. But, even though she could recite from her book about 'stranger danger', she would still go up to any stranger in the street and talk to them. Asking her to go upstairs to fetch two or more items was a mistake, as she would come back with only one of them or come back down having completely forgotten what we'd asked her to do. These contradictory abilities are understandable, in that to perform tasks and conceptualise new ideas you need a well-connected brain and a high level of executive functioning, but if you are constantly in a state of high alert, then being vigilant and detecting changes in your environment is easy.

Another effect of Jemma's early life was physiological and related to poor sensory motor integration. This is the process by which our nerves and muscles work together in a co-ordinated way to facilitate movement, balance and manual dexterity. It gives us bodily control and helps us to know where our body is in space. It gives us hand-to-eye co-ordination and the ability to know left from right. Jemma had been diagnosed with dyslexia by the time she was six, and this was accompanied by a degree of dyspraxia. Her spatial awareness and balance was poor, and she would frequently fall, trip and walk into things.

I had always considered that some of the unusual ways Jemma interpreted sensory information was unique to her until I attended a support group with about 20 other adopters. Three of them said their child had their wiring reversed when it came to touch and temperature. Jemma also displayed these phenomena. On a freezing cold day, she would happily wear just a T-shirt and go without a coat, if she could get away with it, but in the heat of summer would be wrapped in several layers and wearing a hood. She needed any touch to be firm and definite. If you hugged her, you needed to be almost crushing her. She would pull away from any light touch, or accuse you of hurting her. These physiological oddities were also part of her trauma signature. The parents at the support group whose children experienced these sensory impairments also talked about their violence, aggression and general disconnectedness.

Jemma is unique, but she is far from a special case. From speaking with adoption support workers and reading many accounts of adopters' experiences, it appears that a large minority of children placed for adoption each year have a combination of the problems I have described, resulting from abuse experienced in their early years. The impact and consequences of this is now commonly described as developmental trauma disorder, thanks to the work of Bessel van der Kolk and colleagues (2014). Van der Kolk considers that the complex developmental effects of childhood trauma are not captured by the current diagnosis of post-traumatic stress disorder (PTSD) and related conditions. There is need of a better, more precise diagnosis for children with complex histories in order to develop more effective rationales for helping them (van der Kolk, 2005). Getting this universally recognised and accepted is one of the main challenges for adoption now.

Jemma's early existence had left her permanently compromised in many ways. Having an almost non-existent concept of self and a view of others as untrustworthy and unsafe made it all but impossible for her to understand, establish or maintain meaningful relationships. This, I believe, is the most disabling of the consequences of her early upbringing.

There is a well-known saying, 'Birds of a feather flock together.' We most readily associate with people who share our culture, values, preferences and beliefs. We coalesce with those of similar identity. We form tribes. Jemma struggled to make sense of the most basic components of the complex interactions that take place between human beings. She had no sense of who *she* was, let alone anyone else. There were no other people like her in her version of reality, and even if there were, she had no idea how to relate to them.

As a small child, her cute looks and immaturity won a degree of tolerance from adults and older children. They could find her endearing and put up with her outbursts, in small doses at least. This meant that, in some way, others related to her, even if she could not fully relate back. As she grew older, the cuteness became less of a protective factor and, although she could still be charming enough to get along with many adults, she found it hard to establish a meaningful, long-term rapport with anyone, and almost impossible to relate to her peers and make friends. At home, our role as her parents was made equally difficult; what we thought would be a five kilometre fun-run was rapidly turning into a lonely marathon. Despite our best efforts, we found it hard to establish the kind of relationship with Jemma we had hoped for. This was both demoralising and difficult. We so wanted her to become a fully integrated part of our family, to feel one of us, to be part of our 'tribe'. Over time it became clear that she was ill equipped to do this. Her abusive early childhood effectively left her in a tribe of one.

References

Bowlby J (1969). *Attachment and Loss*. London: Hogarth Press.

Dawson P, Guare R (2004). *Executive Skills in Children and Adolescents*. New York: Guilford Press.

Gaensbauer TJ (2002). Representations of trauma in infancy: clinical and theoretical implications for the understanding of early memory. *Infant Mental Health Journal 23*(3): 259–277.

Glaser D (2000). Child abuse and neglect and the brain: a review. *Journal of Child Psychology and Psychiatry 41*(1): 97–116.

Holmes J (1993). *John Bowlby and Attachment Theory*. London: Routledge.

Lansdown R, Burnell A, Allen M (2007). Is it that they won't do it, or is it that they can't? Executive functioning and children who have been fostered and adopted. *Adoption and Fostering 31*(2): 44–53.

Maslow AH (1987). *Motivation and Personality* (3rd ed). Delhi, India: Pearson Education.

Rogers CR (1951). *Client Centred Therapy*. London: Constable.

Rogers CR (1957). The necessary and sufficient conditions of therapeutic personality change. *Journal of Consulting Psychology 21*: 95–103.

Rogers CR (1961). *On Becoming a Person*. New York, NY: Houghton Mifflin.

Van der Kolk B (2005). Developmental trauma disorder: toward a rational diagnosis for children with complex trauma histories. *Psychiatric Annals 35*(5): 401–408.

Van der Kolk B (2014). *The Body Keeps the Score*. London: Penguin.

Winnicott DW (1965). *The Maturational Processes and the Facilitating Environment*. London: Karnac Books.

Chapter 3
Caring for Jemma

My mother's youngest brother, Harry, and his wife, Evelyn, were perhaps the closest members of my extended family. Uncle Harry had often taken me fishing as a child, and I had grown up alongside my two cousins, Martin and Julie. About three months after Jemma was placed with us, Harry and Evelyn celebrated their 40th wedding anniversary. We thought Jemma was probably settled enough by then to introduce her to the wider family. The party was to be held in the small church hall near to where they lived, and provided the perfect opportunity.

When we arrived, things were just getting under way. The outside entrance was festooned with balloons and banners, and the theme continued when we opened the door and stepped into the main hall. Groups of tables and chairs were arranged around an open floor (Harry and Evelyn were great ballroom dancers) and about three-quarters were occupied.

I had been carrying Jemma on one arm up to that point and put her down to give Evelyn a hug. The moment her feet hit the ground, Jemma made a beeline for an elderly man sitting at the table in front of us, climbed onto his lap and just sat there. We stared, motionless for a few seconds. The old chap pulled back his head slightly, smiled and, looking very puzzled, said, 'Oh... hello.' He then turned to us. Anne rushed over, apologised, and removed the misplaced toddler. The man turned out to be a distant cousin on my auntie's side, whom I had never met, and I haven't seen him since.

She may have had only a few words, but Jemma's behaviour was telling us something loud and clear. It was totally at odds with the behaviour that most well-adjusted and securely attached three-year-olds exhibit. It was also nonsensical in terms of how most infants deal with the insecurity of unfamiliar surroundings and, considering Jemma's heightened sense of anxiety and general fearfulness, you would have thought she would be extremely hesitant to go so willingly to a complete stranger.

Like most of the things that small children get up to, everyone at the party thought it was endearing and amusing. For us, it was a shock and a lesson learned. Individual people had no special meaning in Jemma's life, and she had no attachment figures. As such, this kindly looking old gentleman with white hair represented as good a place to sit as anywhere else in the room.

Since birth, she had spent most of her waking hours on high alert, functioning from the primitive region of her brain in response to threat and poor care-giving. The development of emotional attachments in her mid-brain and the cause and effect and meaning-making abilities in her forebrain had been stunted by a lack of the loving human contact required to promote them. Not only was Jemma not attached to anyone, she had not developed the necessary neurological wiring to do so.

For Anne and me, as her parents, this would become a major challenge. We were longing and determined to make her ours, but running alongside that wish was a fundamental expectation that we would be able to build a fully functioning family, of which she was a part and in which we held a special place for her as her mum and dad.

I was very slowly to discover that caring for Jemma and being her parent were both the same and different. To be her parent, I needed to care for her; but in order to care for her, I obviously did not have to be her parent, even though this was what I had set out to be.

The fact that I wanted to care for Jemma as her father was my need and not necessarily hers, and it had not been obvious to me at the outset that being her dad relied so heavily on her. It was not something I could take for granted or impose. It relied on her being able to allow me to parent her, and on me being able to accept the limitations she had in being my daughter and being cared for.

Despite my hopeful vision of what adoption would mean for us as a family and all the effort I put in during those years of completing the application process, it is perhaps clear from this that, as a new adopter, I still didn't really know what I was getting into. It may have been true that, since our first approach to the adoption agency, I had devoured all the information I could find on the exact nature of adoption and adopted children, but I had also retained those hopes and dreams of being a dad again. These had not shifted in the light of all that new information. Rather than putting me off adoption, it had, if anything, become something of a calling. Through adoption we could not only complete our family; we could also be part of a noble enterprise. We could offer a hurt and vulnerable child a good home and an awful lot of love, and I think this played heavily into the rescuer in me.

I think this emotional thinking is common to most first-time adopters, in one form or another. We may take the classes, speak to other adopters and do all the reading, but does that really dampen our enthusiasm or make for a more balanced decision? This is often reflected in the Prospective Adopters Reports (PARs) that support applications for people who want to become adopters. In my experience, there is often a disconnect between their hopes and expectations and what they have been learning in their preparation groups about the realities of adoption.

It might state in one section of an applicant's report, for instance, that:

> They understand the lasting impact of abuse on
> adopted children. They feel they could parent a child

affected by significant neglect and physical violence but would not easily cope with a child who has been sexually abused, although they realise this may only become apparent once a child is settled with them.

And later, in summing up, the report will also say:

They are looking forward to having children placed with them and see themselves in 20 years' time with a loving family around them and hopefully with grandchildren.

These two statements indicate two distinct lines of thinking that do not match and a naïve confidence in their ability to make it all work. When we go on holiday, we take out travel insurance but we don't expect to have to use it. We don't allow ourselves to dwell on the fact that travel comes with certain risks and we focus on the dream that has been the driving force for our pending adventure. As an adopter, I wonder if I was so emotionally bound up in the potential for great things that I got hijacked by my own hope and optimism and was unable to conceive that it could work out anything other than well.

I believe I am not alone in this positivity, and it creates a vulnerability in adopters that is rarely recognised or acknowledged. Perhaps the reality of the risks will only ever feature in our thinking when we have a very damaged and struggling child and are living through the consequences of that for ourselves. There is a section on strengths and vulnerabilities in every PAR but, in my experience, any vulnerabilities are often underplayed and any exploration of them relates to how they might affect the applicants' abilities to parent and do a good-enough job. The fact that the applicants may be vulnerable persons in their own right is not usually considered.

Obviously, every child is different, and there is a spectrum of difficulty that can be experienced in adoptive families. Many adoptions go well, with relatively few problems and, for reasons that are often unclear, some children are less affected by abuse than others and cope better in later life. As our social worker noted, it is a matter of pot-luck.

Thanks primarily to recent advances made in trauma research, we know an increasing amount about the effects of abuse on adopted children, but having this knowledge just helps us to understand things better; it does not reduce the impact of that trauma in terms of their behaviour, their thinking and the challenges they present to being parented. And, although there has been an increasing emphasis on post-adoption support in recent years, this has not reduced the risks or the challenges facing adopters in their daily strivings to parent and care for the children placed with them. The risks and the problems remain firmly at their door.

Our initial attempts to parent Jemma were understandably adapted from the model of parenting we had arrived at with Michael. We had prepared ourselves to adjust that model to take into account the specific needs of children like Jemma. Much of it was instinctive, like the endless games of peek-a-boo and hide-and-seek and desensitising her to the bathroom with crazy water games. We took into account all the advice from our social worker: we developed good routines, provided clear boundaries and containment, let her settle in before exposing her to the rest of the family, spent plenty of quiet time with her, and so on. Most of the practical issues like bath time, eating and sleeping were rapidly dealt with and we learned how to modify our lifestyle to fit around our new family dynamic and Jemma's quirks and requirements. However, screaming and aggression still made up a large part of Jemma's day.

After some initial gains, she made extremely slow progress and we started to think that she had an underlying problem that we needed to locate and resolve in some way. We started searching for the reason why she clearly did not function, behave or fit in as other children did, and so began our involvement with the many professionals and agencies that came under the general headings of health, education and social services.

Although these services are standard for all children, the issues facing adoptees and their parents are often significantly different from those of birth parents. This is not always appreciated by the people working for the various agencies; we only had to take a few steps away from the specialist provision we had from the Family Placement Unit and this, and any relevant understanding of or empathy with what we were experiencing, was lost.

Ironically, adopters are judged on their ability to engage with other services as part of their assessment and are given the message that they will probably need to seek help from them at some point. Based on limited experience, and on what we had been told at adoption preparation classes, we had expected any support would be joined up, with Jemma at the centre. We had thought it would look like this:

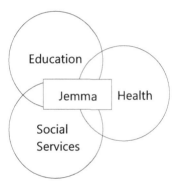

Unfortunately, what we experienced was this:

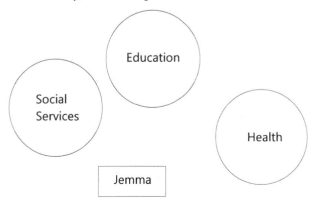

The link between social care, health and education is at best tenuous, and when budgets get squeezed, things can become confrontational rather than collaborative. Even if an air of co-operation is presented at some level, each organisation functions independently of one another and anyone trying to access help can end up bouncing around between them. This is not a revelation to anyone who has been in need of multi-agency working or to those of us who have worked in these services. Despite various edicts from the government and initiatives for change, these three organisms generally return to the same, siloed state.

In a process he called dynamic conservatism, Donald Schon (1971) claimed that organisations have tendencies to actively resist change and fight to stay the same. Under this model, the social system that governs any organisation has a structure (rules and interactions), a technology (tools and techniques) and a theory (value and belief system). Schon defined seven dynamic stages in the resistance to change within organisations. Anyone who has tried to bring about a significant shift in any organisation may well recognise stage 5, where the change agent runs out of energy and gives up, having become disheartened and worn down by the offensive strategies that the organisation has thrown at them, often culminating in it agreeing to change but actually carrying on as before.

Schon does see at least one upside of dynamic conservatism, in that it can prevent organisations from disrupting and tearing themselves apart, although he proposes that they may eventually collapse or become irrelevant at stage 6, after repeated resistance to change. At stage 7, if a transformation has finally been successful and the organisation has moved into a changed state, the agent of change is often metaphorically crucified by the organisation in a course of action termed the messianic process.

I can see how this model is applicable to what we experienced, and how something very like it coloured our contact with the various sub-units and departments in health, education and social care. By advocating for Jemma and challenging their responses, we were, in a way, trying to get these organisations to be different and I think this was often, at some level, construed as a challenge or threat to their social system. This influenced our dealings with officials from all three public services.

Education is an area that causes problems for many adopters and it was always going to be tough for Jemma, and ultimately for us. We went into her school before she started, to give them a booklet on adopted children, how they can present as quirky, to say the least, and how best to help them. We also provided some more specific information about Jemma.

We had found out the hard way that she was a 'bolter'. She had never developed the invisible piece of elastic that connects most young children to their carers. Hence, she would run off without a backwards glance, and we had to constantly keep one eye on her, especially in crowded situations. We told the school this. They said they understood.

On her second day in the reception class, Anne was asked to go in to see the teacher at home time. Apparently, Jemma had run off during lunch break when she was let out into the playground. Fortunately, someone spotted her going out of the gate, gave chase and caught up with her at the end of the road. There was some surprise in the teacher's voice as she explained this and informed Anne that we needed to keep a close eye on Jemma because 'she is likely to run off'.

This was the first time we experienced what was to become a common phenomenon. We would tell a professional something significant about Jemma and at some future point they would tell it back to us as some amazing, new insight into her behaviour.

Based on Schon's model, I think our frequent attempts to impart our knowledge to the professionals put them and the rules of their social system under threat. It is probably not acceptable if the helper, in this case the teacher, learns something from the helpee, as this is a reversal of both the recognised roles and the hierarchy, and would not fit with the theory of their system. Hence, in order to resist this low-level challenge, the system simply ignores it.

We were also very assertive parents, and at times we probably overstepped the mark because we expected the experts to have at least some of the answers. When they didn't, they probably experienced our expectations and our questioning of them as unreasonable and quite critical.

When we began to make even more assertive approaches to the school, it was alarming how quickly Jemma's problem behaviour was laid at our door, with scant reference to her early life. When she acted out, it was because we were not providing firm boundaries, and we were sent on courses to learn to be better parents. When we raised the fact that she was clearly falling behind her peer group in her learning and social interactions, we were told that it was because we (or, more precisely, Anne) were neurotic parents who expected too much of her. These were possibly versions of stages 2 and 3 of dynamic conservatism, in which we were being repelled or contained, and in which any uncomfortable feelings arising in the professionals from our critical feedback were being projected back onto us.

We also encountered a fair amount of stereotyping and dogma, driven by the system's limited beliefs. Not all workers stuck rigidly to these, but they were evident to some degree across all the services, not just education. 'Bad child, bad parent' seemed to be at the heart of it, along with the fixed idea that the root of any child-related problem always lies outside the child. That is to say, if a child is having a problem, then the problem is environmental and, by default, the parents created it. The solution, therefore, is to change the parenting, or even the parents. Little thought is given to what might be going on within the child that could be organic, historic or down to a number of separate issues that cannot simply be resolved. No thought is given to the possibility that the organisation itself could be adding to the problems, either directly or by acts of omission.

Perhaps this is an over-simplification of what became a complicated group dynamic but, regardless of its origin, this attitude was extremely unhelpful to us as newly adoptive parents. It was also insulting at times. In doing our best to care for a very difficult and troubled child, we had hoped for some informed help and support, and instead we were soon hitting brick walls.

To resolve some of the problems, we moved Jemma to a different, much smaller school, with a well-run special needs unit and a different social system, and things began to settle slightly. She began to show that, given the right conditions, she could think and learn, and was soon reading and writing at a basic level. Things were still far from ideal; her behaviour remained a big problem and there was clearly something different about her in comparison with her classmates. We made weekly, and sometimes daily, trips into school to resolve issues of one kind or another, and we soon became accustomed to what many parents know as 'the walk of shame'.

Jemma's school reports always read as if they were about two different children: the teachers who 'got it' painted one picture of her; those who didn't painted another, revealing their lack of understanding of her presentation in their written comments. The latter group could not see why she needed to sit at the back of class to feel safe, insisted that she sat at the front and were mystified when the week-long project on 'My Family' caused her so many problems.

Adopters of very troubled children often experience these kinds of difficulties with education professionals; this is well known. Dealing with it requires broad shoulders and determination. Some adopters are fortunate enough to find schools that are supportive and co-operative and able to understand the particular presentations of these children and take them into account. From hearing many adoption stories, I know this is not the usual experience. There also seems to be a tipping point beyond which initial co-operation fades and the frustration tolerance of the school is exceeded. This probably occurs when the technology (tools and techniques) has all been tried and found wanting and the parents or child present a challenge that questions the theory of the system: 'He seems quite bright, why is he not learning to read... and why is he beating up the dining room staff every day?' Responsibility for the failure to resolve such problems has to be placed somewhere, and it is never with the system itself.

We had similarly varying results with health. Breaking

into the inner circle of the NHS Child and Adolescent Mental Health Services (CAMHS) took some grit and determination, and about two years, during which they would very kindly write to us periodically to check if we still needed an urgent appointment. Once we got through the perimeter fence, our initial interactions with them were disappointing. Jemma's problems were dismissed by the first consultant paediatrician, who wrote in his letter to us that there was basically nothing wrong and 'all she needs is love'. Subsequently we worked our way through several other practitioners who decided there was, after all, something very wrong and, perhaps understandably, each veered towards their own speciality. Hence, she soon acquired a list of diagnoses. When we saw the expert on attention deficit hyperactivity disorder (ADHD), she was diagnosed with ADHD; when we saw the expert on autistic spectrum disorder (ASD), she was diagnosed with ASD, and when we saw the expert on pathological demand avoidance (PDA), she was diagnosed with PDA. By the age of 12, she had accumulated six diagnoses and none of them made complete sense, even to the small care team who were holding her case.

This accumulation of diagnoses is extremely common in children with backgrounds and behaviours like Jemma's. Research papers have been written that explain how this happens, but it still goes on. Most of the diagnostic criteria for these conditions overlap, and it's not hard to see that Jemma could be made to fit a number of them to some degree. Mental health conditions and illnesses are diagnosed in a reductionist way that fits with the medical model. That is to say, they are broken down into sets of symptoms that can be observed, measured and ruled out, eventually leaving only one. This way of doing things works for physical health, because there are a number of physical symptoms, tests and biomarkers that prove or disprove the presence, or absence, of most disease states. In mental health, there are almost none. Diagnosis is based very much on opinion and on a set of criteria that has been decided by a committee. Mental health conditions are not definitive in the same way that medical ones are. They are mostly subjective rather than objective.

We unwittingly fed into this diagnostic madness because we were determined to find out what was wrong with Jemma so we could find a solution and 'fix it'. We pursued this like some sort of Holy Grail. Each new cup brought new hope, but then disappointment.

When things had started to become really difficult, we re-contacted our adoption social worker, Caroline, who arranged for us to be assigned a new social worker from the newly formed Adoption Support Team. She, in turn, had a longstanding relationship with our CAMHS social worker, who had an interest and understanding in adoption and worked with a psychiatrist who had been adopted. This was probably the first time we experienced some meaningful, joined-up, supportive and understanding help from a small team we could trust. They seemed dedicated to helping us and did not blame us or push us away. We weren't always of the same mind, but I knew we could have a meeting, agree or disagree on several points and still have a cup of tea together and part on good terms. Despite our different titles as parent and professional, I saw them as people and they saw me as a person, and we just got on with the task of finding the best help and outcomes for Jemma. It was this small group that helped us through the minefield of multi-agency working.

In our pursuit of a remedy, we tried many approaches and took lots of advice, working our way through whichever parenting strategies applied to Jemma's latest diagnosis. We had periods when things seemed to improve and this gave us hope, and periods where things became almost overwhelming. When Jemma reached secondary school, her behaviour deteriorated to a very marked degree, and she was also getting bigger, of course. Manhandling a stroppy five-year-old who is trying to kick you, without hurting them in any way, is a relatively easy task for a fit and healthy adult. Doing the same with a 12-year-old is not so easy. And it didn't stop at kicks; Jemma now resorted to using household equipment: knives most often, but she also attacked or threatened us with garden implements, irons and bottles, to name just a few.

Most of her aggression was directed at Anne but I also had my share, and usually I was the one who stepped in to keep Anne safe, which meant collateral damage at times.

We would discuss her presentation and the dangers we were trying to deal with at the multidisciplinary team (MDT) meetings that by now took place every couple of months to discuss our case. Representatives of different departments from health, education and social services attended. The professionals' responses would generally be sympathetic and ineffective; the main action point was frequently another meeting or assessment. Sometimes one of the workers would tell us that 'what she is doing isn't personal, you know'. Jemma usually apologised after her outbursts, and I think they were trying to get us to see that the behaviour was a result of her condition and not because she hated us and wanted to hurt us. Anne would usually point out that, whatever might be going on for Jemma in the moment, having a carving knife held to your face certainly feels very personal, as does being pushed downstairs. This point, I think, was never truly heard.

Meeting Jemma on the stairs when she was in an emotionally charged state had become quite hazardous and was what eventually brought us some serious attention from services, because she began to take this behaviour into school. Up until then most of her aggression had been confined to us, but now it spilled over into other settings. One day, during a fracas, she tried to push a teaching assistant down a staircase. Meetings were immediately called by the headmaster, who basically wanted to know what we were going to do about it. The difference in attitude was notable. When she threatened and hurt us, we were not supposed to take it personally; when she began to do the same to teaching staff, it was a very serious concern. There was clearly a pricing system operating in this culture, in which we were of a much lower value.

As part of our ongoing search for an answer, Anne attended a conference at which the key speaker was the psychologist and attachment therapist Greg Keck. As she listened to him, she ran mentally through a checklist of what we were experiencing with

Jemma. For the first time, it all added up. What he described made sense in a way that none of the other attempts to understand Jemma's behaviour had. If this was what lay at the root of her problems, it could potentially also offer a solution.

While attachment and attachment disorder are key phrases in the vocabulary of adoption today, they were still emerging at the turn of the century. Jemma's case had just been allocated to a new paediatrician, who had kept herself up to date with modern advances. She made all the right connections on the very first occasion she met Jemma. We were already convinced this was the underlying cause of pretty much all that we had been experiencing, and in her subsequent letter to us the paediatrician included reactive attachment disorder (RAD) on the list of Jemma's diagnoses. However, it did not replace any of the other six: once a specialist has pronounced their opinion, it is hard to get it rescinded.

Having this information did not change anything immediately. Attachment disorder as a diagnosis was in the same position that dyslexia was in the 1970s. Although we saw the obvious links to Jemma's presentation, this insight was not embraced by all those involved in her care. Many of them had not heard of RAD; there was no specific treatment readily available and some still disputed its existence. They seemed to prefer to work with the possibility that she had ADHD and ASD because they knew about them. Most of the information and research into attachment was coming from America, and Anne, resourceful as ever, began researching and fact-finding for herself.

At home and school, things continued to deteriorate. Daily life became intolerable, and our home was not a safe environment for any of us. It came to the point where we were advised by CAMHS that Jemma needed specialist therapy in a residential unit. I remember that meeting well; the advice came as a stunning blow. Having struggled and fought for 10 years, and having come to love Jemma, it was not now easy to think she might leave home and we might have to let someone else care for her. To, effectively, give her up for her own good was a difficult concept to accept. It conflicted massively with who we were as people and as parents. It did not compute. I was not convinced that this was the best way to help her overcome the effects of her early trauma, and I wondered what this would do to our relationship and what it meant for our ongoing role as her parents.

Despite our reluctance and doubts, eventually we both came round to the idea that we could not cope with Jemma as things were and that this was the best, if not the only, way forward; perhaps we could rescue something from our impossible situation by doing this. So, with the help of our CAMHS workers, we applied for funding for a specialist residential placement that could help Jemma with her attachment and behaviour issues. This went before a management committee, some of whom had been attending our regular multidisciplinary team meetings.

Our anguish turned out to be unwarranted. CAMHS and then the Adoption Support Team made an application for funding on three separate occasions and it was turned down. In the rollercoaster of paradoxical feelings that had surrounded our decision-making, we had not anticipated that what had been recommended to us, and we had accepted against our natural instincts, would be refused. No wonder some of those same managers had been so quiet at our meetings.

We obviously don't know how things would have panned out had this all gone ahead, but I believe this decision denied Jemma an important, life-changing opportunity.

Things continued in an increasingly messy state. A plan was put in place to provide regular respite care for Jemma, ongoing support from CAMHS and a place at a special needs school. It was piecemeal, and involved lots of different people with different agendas, and often they weren't talking to one another so, by default, we ended up chasing someone about something every week. In effect we were case-managing our own case and periodically it would all fall apart, despite our best efforts.

After our funding application was rejected, the head teacher of Jemma's new school was parachuted into our regular multidisciplinary team meetings to placate us with promises of how much help they could give Jemma and how they could turn things around. We had no real choice other than to go along with it but her initial bravado soon turned to dust when she found they had taken on more than they had bargained for. Surprise, surprise, Jemma was not autistic and did not behave like the other children in the school. She was repeatedly excluded and segregated, sometimes officially and sometimes unofficially. When this happened, we were asked to go and collect her. I was in a relatively high-pressure management job at the time but luckily I had chosen my staff well and my employers were sympathetic. I began taking time off, either because I was unwell or to deal with regular incidents or attend meetings, and sometimes to be at home to protect Anne. I was allowed to take unpaid leave for a while, but eventually I moved to a different job with shorter hours. Jemma's distress and daily acts of aggression were making life intolerable, and I woke every morning with a sense of dread at what that day might bring and fantasising about packing our bags and running away.

Our excellent respite foster carers saved us from going over the edge. We had not really wanted to place Jemma in respite care, because it clashed with our sense of duty and responsibility as parents, but we were barely functioning. Had we not taken this help, I think we would have sunk. Jemma was like an ocean-going liner, cruising ahead at full steam while we were being tossed about in a rowing boat in the wake of her passage. What she was doing, of course, was recreating the chaos and danger of her early life, and we were powerless to stop her. Regardless of the number of times we supported her, forgave her and reclaimed her, and regardless of our consistent attempts to contain her emotionally, she was responding to life using the script that was her ingrained fall-back position.

Life is difficult for most teenagers and it is especially tricky for traumatised, adopted teenagers. Identity, independence, expectations and hormones come together in a volatile and potentially explosive mix. Under these mounting stressors, any slight progress Jemma may have been making in terms of feeling safe, secure and loved were overwhelmed, and she reverted to the anxious, frightened toddler who had learned that particular way of being. She acted out her fear as uncontrollable anger and aggression. It made sense to her on an unconscious level, even if it didn't on any another.

Jemma had arrived with Sophie, her doll, and we fundamentally understood the relevance of this as a means of comfort: her transitional object, her security blanket. I've described already how, when we saw how attached she was to the doll, we bought a duplicate in case it was ever lost. We had no idea she would retain this need way beyond early childhood. As a teenager, she still carried a doll, by this time replaced by a bigger, better model but nonetheless serving the same purpose. Even though she was now 14, she was not embarrassed to carry it around town, give it its own separate seat in a restaurant or push it to the local shop in a buggy.

The use of a transitional object, whether it be a doll, teddy or blanket, is observed in most children, but only given meaning by the work of Donald Winnicott. He observed that the object becomes a way in which an infant can find comfort as she gradually becomes aware of being separate to her mother and moves towards independence, while hanging on to the safety of the illusion that she is still one with her (Winnicott, 1971; Gomez, 1997). In her obsessive holding of this comfort object, the child seems to have things both ways, and is supported in this strategy by parents and carers who assist this by making the object always available. A key feature of this is that the child can have total power over the object, hugging and snuggling and abusing and treating it roughly, but never to the point of annihilation.

This primitive type of relating has features of what adults would identify as love or hate, but for the child it is far less resolved. Winnicott sees them both as different aspects of the primitive, self-obsessed and ruthless ways a child relates to her world. It is only when the infant comes to realise that her teddy or blanket, the object of her love and hate, is vulnerable and capable of being hurt that the two contrasting feelings become resolved. Winnicott refers to this achievement as 'the stage of concern'. At this point the child begins to learn that an alternative to power and anger can be found in reparation and relationship and she starts to learn to take responsibility for the effect she has on others. This concern for herself and for others can only develop if she has felt safe and has been protected from distress in early life by good care-givers. If she has not experienced this security, she will not be able to move on to trust herself and the adults around her and will instead to hold onto the illusions of her early life.

In a well-cared-for and well-adjusted child, teddy becomes less and less important and over time is gradually replaced by other objects and experiences through which the child can complete her transition to independence. Jemma did not achieve this fundamental transition, and her doll was testimony to that fact. This early failure was key to how her chronological, cognitive and emotional ages then began to diverge. The lack of completion of this stage in her development influenced her thoughts, emotions and behaviour, and delayed her progress.

The far-reaching effects of this were highlighted to me one Friday afternoon when I was taking her to her respite carers for the weekend. As always, she was upset and didn't want to go, and I was trying to contain my guilt and do a selling job at the same time. In the confines of the moving car she would often feel contained enough to talk openly, and she voiced her fear and belief that, while she was away from us over the weekend, we would not be her parents any more. I was dumbfounded by this disclosure and did my best to reassure her and genuinely show my shock and concern. Her fear was so great, and her sense of permanency so weak, that she could not grasp the fundamental concept that, even when she was not with us, we were still her parents. Like a baby who has to learn that their parents still exist even when they move out of sight, she had needed to learn that we were not like the many mummies and daddies she had met before us. We were not going to disappear. We were forever. The fact that she had not managed to internalise this concept was a revelation that still sits with me. She had been with us for more than 10 years and yet this was not part of her thinking. We had not done enough to convince her that we were a permanent part of her life and she seemed stuck with the same internal working model that she had arrived with. It gives some indication of how her object constancy had been skewed and how very different her understanding of the world was from mine.

Given this, it's easy to see why she hated to go away from us so much; I don't like to dwell on what she must have been feeling at those times when, in her mind at least, we abandoned her. The level of uncertainty and fear she must have been living with is too painful to contemplate.

It also goes part way to explain why parenting her had been so hard, to the point at which I often felt I was no longer her parent and had shifted into purely a carer's role or, even worse, a containment role. And even that was becoming precarious, as we were continually locked in a round of challenges and rows, with both physical and verbal battles on an almost daily basis.

Her behaviour had become antisocial. In most families where children have been cared for, have generally met their milestones and have gone through all of the major developmental stages from within the security of a loving, caring environment, antisocial tendencies can be resolved within the family unit. Most parents intuitively know what to do to restore order, trust and confidence in their teenage offspring. For Jemma, the turmoil and chaos of her inner world had never been resolved, so there *was* nothing to be restored; she had never fully resolved issues of object constancy, love and hate and independence.

This also largely explains why, up to the age of nine or 10, she would get upset and angry that Anne could not personally feel her pain if Jemma hurt herself. Whenever she fell or bumped herself, she would place Anne's hand on the injury and expect her to physically feel the pain. We had no idea that this was a clear indication that she had not fully made the transition from the illusion of being one with her mother. As Anne was not her biological mother, this must have been doubly confusing for Jemma and probably played into her doubts about mothers as reliable and caring attachment figures.

In retrospect, I can see how we may have unconsciously been drawn into Jemma's infantile way of being. All through her teenage years, Anne and I would sometimes still use Jemma's pet name, 'the baby', when talking about her to one another, and this was perhaps indicative of our unconscious relating to her as the unresolved, omnipotent child. This was still how she behaved. When overwhelmed by the fear that accompanied her primitive feelings, she would act them out in some way, in a frantic attempt to have them contained by those around her. Just as a baby will scream when it is hungry or needs its nappy changing, Jemma would shout or hit out to try to remain in charge of her world, in the expectation that her fear of annihilation would be alleviated. She was assuming the all-powerful position of the omnipotent child. She was speaking to us through her aggressive behaviour but unfortunately, because we had not spotted, let alone been able to bridge, the very fundamental gaps in her development, we did not know how to meet those needs in a way that stopped them recurring and so we kept reliving the same trauma. Behaving antisocially made unconscious sense to Jemma; it perversely brought her some relief because it allowed her to externalise her inner anxiety and fear of annihilation. She was trapped in this infantile way of relating, looking for containment and, when she could not find it, simply escalating her behaviour.

This was central to how our parenting and care of her evolved and how we functioned as a family. Unfortunately, our initial belief that, if we could just be good and dedicated parents, it would help Jemma overcome her trauma, was fatally flawed. Simply providing the generally accepted regimes of good parenting was never going to cut it for Jemma. She was not a blank sheet and nor was she equipped to be parented in a traditional way. Our attempts to find a solution to her difficulties had in fact not just been dead ends; they had only added to her distress. When we had followed the advice on how to parent children with ADHD, for instance, it included elements of isolating and ignoring her. This compounded her anxiety and reinforced her sense of hopelessness. It affirmed her view that she was a bad person and out of control. It did not convince her of any need for reparation or conformity because she was literally unable to grasp those concepts. When we used rewards for good behaviour, we had not understood that working towards a reward required her to believe she was a good enough person to receive it in the first place and trust that it was achievable and would happen. Jemma held neither of these beliefs, and we soon learned the futility of star charts.

We had made similar failed attempts with other ideas and models as she grew up. Added to this, the increasing involvement of statutory services brought with it an increasing number of assessments and tests. Then there was school and the multitude of negative messages she received from teachers and peers, most of whom understood her as little as she understood them; they just scared the living daylights out of one another.

Throughout her childhood, Jemma received a barrage of negative messages that, according to Bowlby's theories (outlined in Chapter 2), would reinforce her internal working model of herself as worthless and the world as a hostile place. They brought with them negative conditions of worth that, from a person-centred perspective, would have prevented or even destroyed any positive growth.

This is where, for me, object relations and person-centred theories converge to tell me the same thing, using slightly different terminology. Carl Rogers (1961) believed that to be fully functional was to be in process, moving towards something new that we would become and in which we could be fully ourselves. He termed this process actualisation. The urge to expand, develop and mature as human beings is within all of us, and we can do this when we are in an authentically genuine relationship in which we experience conditions of empathic, warm and non-judgmental acceptance. He coined the term 'unconditional positive regard', where we experience no conditions of worth and are simply valued for who we are, and not judged.

Although Rogers focused on the creative and positive side of human beings in his theories, other workers have extended these ideas to look at how actualisation can go in more than one direction.

Robert Carkhuff postulated that the absence of Rogers' conditions at key moments or points of crisis could be disastrous and lead to deterioration (Carkhuff, 1987; Brazier, 1996). These theories suggest that we are all born with our actualising tendency intact but this is eroded by conditions of worth that are placed on us in many settings, such as home, school and religious groups. These conditions imply that I am only good enough if I meet certain requirements, and if I don't, then I am a failing, or even a bad person. At any stage of life, these can be destructive.

Society is full of such conditions, which come in many different versions and contribute to a world that is full of tribes, each with its own rules, values and beliefs. Given Jemma's sense of how the world worked and where she fitted into it, she was not equipped to meet many of the conditional requirements placed on her. For instance, the tribe called school wanted well-behaved students who contributed to the endeavours of the school by learning and achieving good grades. She could do none of this and was frequently excluded, in many ways, and got the very clear message that she was bad and stupid and doomed to failure.

From the psychoanalytic perspective of Winnicott, Jemma's weak sense of true self – so weak that as a toddler she could not recognise herself in a mirror – was overwritten by an unhealthy sense of false self. Jemma had generated this false self in response to her multiple privations, in an attempt to protect herself from the fear of annihilation when her needs were not met. She probably never felt safe enough throughout her first two years of life to be able to find and develop any sense of true self that was unintegrated and independent of her mother. Her trauma had disrupted her normal development so much that it left her stuck with many remnants of an infantile way of relating and prevented her from creating a false self that would be of any help to her going forward. Her failure at this critical developmental stage stopped her reaching subsequent stages of development successfully and left her ill equipped to relate to the world and other people in a way that had meaning to her, or to those around her. Navigating the world from this position is rather like trying to drive a 30-ton truck in heavy traffic when you've never even managed to start a car successfully. This was the basis from which she grew into deficit.

Whether considering Jemma from a psychological perspective using the theories of Winnicott, Bowlby or Rogers, I am drawn to the same overriding conclusion: psychologically, she was totally unprepared for life in the world, to learn from it, negotiate its many winding paths or fit into its complex structures. She was emotionally and psychologically disabled.

On some level, Anne and I gradually came to understand this, even before we had the knowledge and information to support any specific theory. This was something we had not planned or wanted when we first decided to adopt. In the preparation and matching process, we had looked closely at what we felt we could cope with, and one thing on our 'No' list was a child with a significant disability who would not be able to reach independence. We wanted, needed even, a child who would simply grow up and become an adult. For Jemma, this was a tall order.

In his book *The Body Keeps the Score*, trauma expert Bessel van der Kolk (2014) describes and provides evidence for how trauma in very early life impairs brain development and is laid down as a body memory. It affects the entire human organism, affecting just about every area of functioning. He talks about how, after trauma, the world is experienced differently, with an altered nervous system and with immune systems, stress hormones and all aspects of development affected. While her attachment issues underpinned most of Jemma's behaviour towards us, this thinking brought together just about everything we understood and had experienced as her parents. Regrettably, yet again, having the knowledge and making it count towards getting help for her were two very separate things; the latter did not flow automatically from the first.

By adolescence, Jemma showed no progress and no sign of giving up her routine outbursts. We developed a way of existing that provided some very limited kind of daily life, in which almost everything was geared towards her needs, and we became very isolated. Her new school had pretty much given up. Whether out of embarrassment, pity or a fear of the consequences for them should one of us be seriously hurt, the local authority managers agreed joint funding with health for some family therapy at a leading third sector organisation that specialised in adoption and attachment.

This was a turning point in how we managed to care for Jemma and function as a family. We were assigned a team of therapists, an educationalist, an occupational therapist and a mentor. They searched Jemma's files for clues, enough to draw up a trauma timeline of her abusive and disrupted early childhood and to match her life events with the key stages in infant development. From this, they were able to make some informed hunches about how specific incidents in her early life would have coincided with and affected certain critical phases.

We learned about our own attachment styles and how Jemma's behaviour triggered our personal responses to her as parents and carers. We looked again at our 'red buttons' and the ways we reacted to the many things she threw at us. We realised that flying bottles leave an emotional dent long after any physical impact has been avoided. We had considered some of these things during our adoption assessment but this time it was with the advantage of seeing them in the context of real experience. Above all, we were heard by the team. We didn't have to explain how bad it was. They just knew. This validation alone was a significant part of the therapeutic process for me.

Caring for Jemma had been a very lonely experience at times, and my life as an adoptive parent has continued to be quite isolating. There are common themes that emerge whenever I talk to other people about Jemma and her problems. Perhaps the most common is their shock and surprise when I say how young she was when we adopted her. Even if they don't voice it explicitly, I often observe their sceptical responses and raised eyebrows. How can someone who was placed as a toddler still be so affected by her early life (assuming we had done all the right things as parents since then)? It makes no sense.

Sometimes they will express their surprise out loud, which at least gives me the chance to talk about it in more depth and explain it as best I can.

I then watch them glaze over as I try to describe it in words of one syllable. It's not easy for me or for them. For someone brought up on the receiving end of good-enough parenting, it requires a complete rethink to fully grasp how abuse shapes a baby's neurological and psychological development and how this can have an ongoing impact. Most people find it hard to comprehend how, by the age of two, Jemma's early existence had left her permanently compromised in many ways, including learning, behaviour and forming relationships.

She was effectively trapped in her trauma, each new experience confirming her past ones in some way or another. The therapy team understood this, and they understood Jemma.

Therapy came thick and fast, and intensively. We started with five days in a row, and then moved onto weekly sessions that lasted a whole day. There was a contract drawn up between us all in which one key point was 'no secrets'. This did not mean Jemma was denied time on her own in therapy or any privacy, but the focus was on relationship and on us becoming family, and in helping us to help her. The team were well aware of the potential for splitting and manipulation by Jemma and their long-term objective was for us to become therapeutic parents. They seemed to have no inflated idea of where they sat within this dynamic: working therapeutically with Jemma alone was not going to be enough; this needed to be a corporate enterprise aimed at providing us all with a way to function as a family.

I imagine many therapists would find this set-up unusual. I have never worked as a therapist with children but as an adoptive parent I am often perplexed when adopters and long-term foster carers tell me they have been completely removed from the therapeutic process, other than taxiing their child to and from appointments. In one such case, my friends Bob and Jane had a near miss when their child went to bed one evening following a therapy session and set fire to the bedroom. Fortunately, no one was harmed, thanks to a very sensitive smoke detector, but this highlights the dangers of isolating carers from the care of their children. Bob and Jane knew their child much better than the therapist did and had they known what had been talked about that day, their sensitivity to the potentially catastrophic consequences of the session would have worked much better than any smoke detector. Given the opportunity, they would have forecast the risks and managed them appropriately.

I am well aware of the 1982 Gillick case and the consequent Fraser guidelines, which establish in law the right of children aged under 16 to make decisions for themselves and have their confidentiality respected, provided they are deemed to have maturity and understanding (BAILII, 1985). I also understand that, where there are safeguarding concerns, confidentiality becomes a crucial issue. However, when there were no such concerns for this child, I cannot see how the therapist thought this way of working was a good idea. Remedy was more likely to come from the child's relationship with Bob and Jane than from two hours a week in therapy, and it's a pity the two could not have been joined up in some way. This could have helped the therapeutic process.

Bob and Jane's experience was very different to ours with Jemma at this time. I really felt held, supported and valued, and it enabled me to examine myself, my parenting of Jemma and the ways we had become stuck and worn down by the daily onslaught of demanding and dangerous behaviour.

Thinking about my own upbringing and history in this therapeutic setting, I was able to identify how and why certain aspects of Jemma's behaviour triggered me so much and find a way of caring for her that was more conducive to de-escalating situations rather than escalating them. We learned about an approach devised by the child psychologist Dan Hughes (Golding & Hughes, 2012) using PACE – playfulness, acceptance, curiosity, empathy – as a way to interact with her, and this began to pay dividends.

Alongside this, the therapy team set about helping Jemma to understand her own life story and work through some of the feelings she previously could not locate or verbalise. In the early stages, she did this from beneath a blanket or spoke with the help of one of the many cuddly toys that were on hand in the therapy rooms. She was allowed to regress and access some of the stages of development she had missed, encouraged to drink from a bottle and become the baby again, but this time within a safe, caring and containing environment.

Even with all this help, life was still very difficult for all of us. Dan Hughes and Jonathan Baylin introduced the concept of blocked care in their book *Brain-Based Parenting* (Hughes & Baylin, 2012), which in part explains how families succumb to the overwhelming challenges they meet when trying to care for very damaged children. Looking back, I think this is what had happened to us.

There were many instances when we were pushed to breaking point. One Saturday morning, just before the therapy began, having caused havoc at the breakfast table, Jemma stormed out of the room. I followed her into the hall, only to be showered with wet scrambled egg and chewed toast that she had stored in her mouth and then spat all over me as she ran upstairs. I chased after her, which on reflection was not the best thing to do, and she slammed her bedroom door shut and proceeded to kick it with such force that one of the bottom panels shot out and across the landing, leaving a hole like a giant cat-flap. At this stage, my 'parenting brain' was not functioning all that well and, frankly, I wanted to throttle her.

That day, things did calm down and we went through our usual apology and reclaiming process and got on with the day, but danger was never very far away. Later, while trying to do 'nice things' in the garden, Jemma broke a large terracotta pot and, although I only said, 'Oh, Jemma, do be careful', this caused a massive reaction. She stormed off into the house, picked up a knife and threatened to stab Anne. This seemingly small garden accident had sparked an immense sense of rejection in her. The disproportionate hurt and anger she experienced as a result had to be directed at someone, and Anne, as mother figure, was the obvious choice.

This was just an average Saturday and there were incidents like this every week. Many of them were seriously dangerous. Under these conditions, being a good parent, as the world might see it, and not activating my own self-defence system, was very hard.

My parenting had become reactive and was based on just getting through each day or surviving each incident in the day. Any effective communication between Jemma and me was not possible when she was in full flight-and-fight mode, and all I could do was react to the immediate threat. She then perceived a counter-threat from me and a lot of shouting would go on. Her mood could change from moment to moment, as if at the flick of a switch, and I could not keep up with these sudden swings. Often, by the time I was getting back to feeling okay, it all kicked off again. If Anne or I were pushed to our absolute limit, we would simply leave the situation and the other would take over. The house was never at peace, and the bar was pushed higher each time we went through one of these cycles.

Hughes and Baylin postulate that there are five parenting systems that make up the parenting brain. One of these, the parental reward system, is a natural part of the bonding process that takes place between parents and their children. Jemma was unable to respond to me as her father, and sometimes not even as her carer, and, combined with her aggressive behaviour, this had engendered a sense of hopelessness and resentment in me. I also felt unsafe and out of control, mimicking her emotional state. I think my parenting brain was well and truly turned off.

Under the terms Hughes and Baylin employ, we were most probably experiencing child-specific and stage-specific blocked care by the time we got into therapy and had been doing so for some time. We had managed to stay receptive and undefended towards Jemma for most of her early childhood but as her behaviour deteriorated in her teenage years, due to that explosive mix of identity, independence, expectations and hormones, I had become more and more sensitised. I was brought up in a relatively quiet, calm and secure household, where most disputes were settled by Mum laying down the law and Dad just smiling and lighting another Woodbine. I do not deal easily with confrontation. I hate it and generally avoid it. Having to face the out-and-out aggression we received from Jemma on a daily basis triggered my limbic system and sent me hurtling into defence mode and away from care-giving mode.

This slowly began to change once we started therapy. We were supported to continue the work with Jemma between sessions and care for her in a very different way. Being supported and not blamed was an essential component of this change, as we set about using the Dan Hughes model, stepped away from just dealing with Jemma's behaviour and tried to see it as a language from which we could learn. Her angry outbursts were communicating something; it all had meaning and we began to learn how to respond, rather than react. So, when she sat violently kicking the table leg at dinner, instead of bluntly telling her to stop as it was annoying and damaging the table, we would, in an interested and playful voice, say something like, 'Wow Jemma, it seems like you are really wound up about something. I wonder what is stressing you out? I wonder if you're kicking the table like that because you're worried about school tomorrow? Seems like you're finding life really tough today.'

Ideally, this new approach using PACE needed to be consistent in all of Jemma's life experiences and not just when she was at home with us. Our respite carers soon came on board with this idea and we worked as a team. The school, too, initially seemed keen to learn about it but then told us that this way of working did not fit with the way the school operated. It was probably too alien for them to comfortably integrate into their social system.

Despite this setback, over a period of about six months, we began to see noticeable changes in all of us. Life was still very hard and Jemma's behaviour continued to be challenging in a range of settings, underpinned at home by her attachment problems, in which she desperately wanted us and also had a pathological need to reject us. However, things were gradually getting noticeably better and Jemma had stopped trying to seriously harm Anne. Being able to do quite simple things like use a sharp knife in the kitchen and pass Jemma safely on the stairs was a real benefit to our daily lives. She also began to have good eye contact with Anne, which she had never done before.

There was a faint light at the end of the tunnel and, for the first time in years, we seemed to have something that worked and to be going forward in some areas. Armed with the right tools and support, it seemed like we now at least stood a chance.

References

Brazier DD (1996). *The Post-Rogerian Therapy of Robert Carkhuff.* [Online.] Malvern: Amida Trust. www.academia.edu/3663201/The_Post-Rogerian_Therapy_of_Robert_Carkhuff (accessed 17 April 2018).

British and Irish Legal Information Institute (BAILII). *Gillick v West Norfolk & Wisbech Area Health Authority (1985) UKHL 7.* [Online.] www.bailii.org/uk/cases/UKHL/1985/7.html (accessed 17 April 2018).

Carkhuff RR (1987). *The Art of Helping.* Amherst, MA: Human Resource Development Press.

Golding KS, Hughes DA (2012). *Creating Loving Attachments.* London: Jessica Kingsley.

Gomez L (1997). *An Introduction to Object Relations.* London: Free Association Books.

Hughes DA, Baylin J (2012). *Brain-Based Parenting.* New York, NY: WW Norton & Co.

Rogers CR (1961). *On Becoming a Person.* New York, NY: Houghton Mifflin.

Schon DA (1971). *Beyond the Stable State.* New York, NY: WW Norton & Co.

Van der Kolk B (2014). *The Body Keeps the Score.* London: Penguin.

Winnicott D (1971). *Playing and Reality.* London: Tavistock.

Chapter 4
Success and failure

When Jemma was 10, we bought her a pet rabbit. She had been asking to have one for ages but our previous attempts with a hamster and a gerbil had both ended in The Great Escape, so we weren't sure how successful this would be. I had visions of repeatedly chasing the creature around the garden, trying to catch it. As it turned out, the rabbit was a great success; Jemma loved little Barney to the point where we regularly had to remind her that he needed at least some time in his cage each day. Barney reciprocated by just being there, totally submissive and accepting of the constant cuddles and pieces of carrot, and always waiting at the front of his run to be claimed and handled. We were encouraged that Jemma could be so loving and attentive. This caring side of her personality also extended to very small children and anyone she could mother, even though she struggled in her relationships with most of her peers.

There were other ways in which she showed that she could be kind, and even empathic, which came through mostly when she was under no perceived threat and was feeling in control of the situation. Many of the people who knew us and Jemma would speak of these qualities when things were not going well, pointing out that it was our influence on her that made her this way. It was some acknowledgement of success for her and for us.

As Jemma got older we needed reminding of this often. Until she started senior school, things had been difficult but manageable; we ticked along, dealing with regular crises and remaining optimistic. In the difficult and often chaotic years of her early teens, it was hard to fathom what any of us were getting out of this life together. Much of the time it was pretty fraught and not the joyful experience we had hoped for.

Thinking in terms of success and failure in relation to adoption seems inappropriate in many ways. How do you measure it, for one thing? Even if you could, I am not sure it would be helpful and the answer would surely depend on who you are and where you are standing, and it could also vary over time. And what would it really mean? When it comes down to it, do we think of our families in that way? It seems almost immoral.

Those two words, success and failure, seem to fall in with ideas such as right and wrong, good and bad. As a person-centred therapist, I always try to be careful when using such terms. I often meet clients who come to counselling because they are struggling with dilemmas in which they are frantically searching for the right answer, only to find that their dilemma is really a paradox and there is no right or wrong, just different choices. In my experience, much of life is like that.

I have no doubt that Jemma would give a positive testimonial about her time with Barney but I wouldn't assume to know how she feels about the wider picture of her life with us. I am not even sure she would know that herself, or be able to give a clear verdict on the subject.

A couple of years ago, I worked briefly with a young man who had been adopted. He was in his late 20s and, considering his very rocky start in life, was doing quite well. He had a long-term partner and a baby, and had managed to find work for most of his adult life, although he had never settled in one place for long. He told me that he had a great childhood in his adoptive home but left when he was 18 as they had all 'had enough of each other'. He still saw his adoptive parents infrequently but his relationship with them was not good. He was very clear and not at all fazed by the idea that his adoption had been both a good experience and a bad one. Even though he would have preferred things to be different, he seemed to have accepted this paradox on some level.

From an adopter's perspective, this subjective response does not seem surprising. It is perhaps indicative of someone looking at adoption from the inside out and reflects its many contrasting and paradoxical experiences. Those observing adoption from the outside in, I find, usually want to be more objective in their assessment of it.

The ways in which this is done and the measures used to determine success or failure seem to depend on the underlying agenda of the person or groups in question. For instance, the government looks for performance-related measures that are primarily statistical and based on societal, financial or political needs. Currently, these needs seem to be associated with an underlying ethos that adoption is a good and effective way to look after children who can no longer live with their family of birth. Once that belief is accepted as a truth, several questions arise. How many children have been adopted, are waiting or are looked after in some other way? How long have they been in care? How much is it costing? Is this causing a problem that we need to focus on? Statistics are compiled by civil servants to provide answers to these questions and provide an objective measurement of success or indicate areas that need attention.

If we consider the view from a local government perspective, similar factors apply, but they are augmented by local needs and agendas. These might mean also taking into account factors such as local or regional variations, pressures on local resources and recent bad press about children's services. Success and failure might also be based on comparative measures – how the area's performance compares with national statistics, for instance, or with other areas, or how well it is meeting current government objectives.

The picture would be incomplete without mentioning the financial element of adoption, because the systems and organisations that manage the adoption process operate within a business economy. Money changes hands between stakeholders at various stages of the process because recruiting, assessing and approving adopters involves a significant amount of time and expense, and agencies need payment for their services in order to survive and continue doing their job. It also costs a lot to keep children in care, and there is an obvious interplay between these two aspects. This economy provides an added dimension to the measurement of success in some quarters.

In 2013 the government announced the availability of a £150 million Adoption Reform Grant to local authorities and a further £15 million to voluntary adoption agencies to expand services and recruit more adopters. Scorecards were also introduced to provide measures of success at local level. Then, in spring 2016, the Department for Education (DfE) (2016a) set out a four-year strategy for adoption in *Adoption: a vision for change*. This outlined the government's ongoing mission to address stumbling blocks to adoption identified in the preceding years and promised a more joined-up approach and the establishment of Regional Adoption Agencies. The report generally built on the view that adoption, as a concept, is something to be encouraged, supported and improved upon and that there were several areas still needing attention. Most of the measures used as indicators of success were understandably statistical, but the report did introduce some potentially subjective measures, not least the establishment of the 'adopter voice as a driver of reform'. It noted changes and improvements required in mental health and education so that those services would acknowledge and make provision for the special needs of adopted children. It also underlined the importance of post-adoption support by increasing and extending the Adoption Support Fund, which was rolled out to all local authorities in 2015 to fund therapy for children.

While all this was very welcome, the underlying message of the strategy was the need to speed things up, make adoption easier and more accessible. 'Recruiting enough adopters to meet the needs of the children waiting' was a theme from previous initiatives, and this was central to many of the changes the government proposed again here. It applied a data-led approach to measuring and managing success, helped in part by the adoption scorecards introduced in 2013. The importance of a child's underlying psychology and attachment in terms of matching got a very brief mention, as did the importance of permanency until the age of 18. There was also a brief reference to post-adoption statistics and future outcomes for adopted children and their families.

This brings me back to the original question of success or failure in adoption. Can it be defined in some way by the speed and number of placements? I imagine that, from the outside, it all seems quite straightforward. The government tells us of the virtues of adoption and its agenda is backed up by reports from some adoption charities that only three per cent of adoptions disrupt. To anyone wanting to adopt a child, this would indicate that the only thing getting in the way of their 'dream family' are the courts and social workers. Taking children out of the care system also brings financial rewards and the impact assessment of the Children and Social Work Bill, published in May 2016 (DfE, 2016b), suggested 'possible savings of £310 million across the whole sector'. Would this not be a measure of success for the government and the taxpayer?

On the ground, things are often different. Adoption workers have never been individually responsible for the perceived delays in the system and have had to work through frequent changes and new policies, even when they have not been persuaded by the underlying arguments. Statistical measures of success have to feature in their thinking, even if these are not their main priority, and they are inevitably influenced by government and local agendas and by whichever agency employs them. However, in addition to this, I believe subjective measures and the needs of individuals, rather than the bigger adoption picture, are largely what influence most workers' thinking. Actually, getting to know adopters and children is very different from working with statistics, theories and policies and the expectations of employers; having to juggle all these competing demands must be difficult. Relating to real people involves an emotional commitment and, although some feelings of success may well come from meeting an agency or government target,

I believe they are more likely to result from removing a child from the care system and helping a childless adopter achieve their dream of having a family. I know many social workers who are dedicated to this purpose and, for them, success and failure have an added dimension, a very personal one.

As an adopter, looking at adoption from the inside, I also have some very personal measures of success and failure. These are mostly subjective and quite ill defined, and are definitely not built on numbers or statistics. If it is possible to separate them out and categorise them, they probably fall into two areas: success for Jemma and success for Anne and me. Even then, who am I to say whether our parenting of Jemma was a success? That remains a question for her. All I can do is reflect on my own sense of how I did as her adoptive dad and how it turned out for me.

When considering how best to help abused and traumatised children, the analogy of them being in a deep hole and needing a ladder to be lowered down to them is sometimes used. This alludes to the fact that they can't change things on their own, they need help. I think I would go one step further in the case of children like Jemma, where the effects of abuse are so fundamental and severe that the child seems to kick away any offer of help, time and time again. It was no use handing Jemma a ladder – she didn't know what ladders were, let alone how to use one, and there were times when she probably perceived them as yet another threat. What she perhaps needed most was for me to jump into the hole with all the wood and nails so we could work out how to make a ladder and escape together. This would be a high-risk strategy as we could both be stuck in the hole forever and, while I like to think I would be prepared to attempt to rescue her in this way, I am not certain I had this level of sacrifice in mind when we adopted her.

In essence, I probably fell short in providing what she needed, although the hole she was in was so deep and confusing I find it hard to imagine that there would be many people on the planet who could have helped her out of it. Had I been aware of everything I now know, things may have worked out differently, but reliving the past 20 years is not an option. I have an idea that the outcomes would have been fairly similar whatever we did. We read all the books, took all the advice and engaged in all the therapy. We tried all the recommended parenting techniques in our attempts to manage Jemma's behaviour and repair some of the damage. Whatever we did only seemed to scratch the surface. She was confrontational, angry and aggressive most of the time, and I find it hard to believe I would ever have had the stamina and fortitude to remain the calm, thoughtful, effective parent I needed to be. The conflict she was so good at creating and perpetuating gradually wore me down.

Jemma may be unique, but she is not alone in her degree of disturbance and in how it disrupts her life. There are thousands of families like ours across the UK. No one really knows how many because the post-adoption data that would show this are not collected and there have been no national, long-term studies of adoption and adopted people. As previously discussed, the statistical information available records practical measures of how many children there are in care, how long they have been there, how many have been placed for adoption, and so on. In the field of adoption, it is well known that many adoptive families face serious difficulties, but there is little qualitative data and no one puts a precise number on how many adoptions break down. There have been studies looking at specific aspects of adoption and there are limited, relatively unreliable numbers collected for administrative purposes. Some workers have attempted to pull all this disparate information together to provide a clearer view of adoption, but with limited success. The first large study of adoption outcomes in the UK, *Beyond the Adoption Order: challenges, interventions and adoption disruption*, by Selwyn, Wijedasa and Meakings, reported in 2014, and this has provided a valuable insight into adoption in the first part of the 21st century. In my view, all prospective adopters should read this report and take note.

The study used a sample of 390 families in which 689 children had been placed from 77 local authorities. Considering the large numbers of children adopted each year (4,690 in

2016), this is a relatively small sample but big enough to give a good insight into the overall picture and to provide a qualitative measure of outcomes and not just quantities.

Just over a third of the adopters in the study reported they had no or few problems and were experiencing what they considered to be a normal family life, 'very similar to many other families in the community'. An approximately equal number reported exactly the opposite, with major life-changing problems and adoption breakdown being common. The group in the middle had experienced 'highs and lows, but mainly highs'.

Many people might see these findings as rather shocking, although those of us who have been adopters for some time, with very damaged and hard-to-care-for children, will probably not be surprised. Our adoption of Jemma would clearly fall into the third of adopters in this survey who experienced serious problems. In 2015 more than 69,000 children were in the care of local authorities and just over 3,300 of them were placed in adoptive homes (about five per cent). If the Selwyn study findings are correct and extrapolated across that population, about 1,000 of those placements will, at some point in the future, result in the same level of heartache and difficulty that we have experienced. This effect is obviously accumulative and, assuming the overall numbers stay the same, another 1,000 families will join that group in each successive year. This is a sizeable minority and fits with my own experience of adoption as a parent and as a professional who knows many other adopters.

There are some pitfalls in looking at the numbers in this way. For one thing, while these categories are helpful for descriptive and data-handling purposes, they obscure the fact that there is a continuum of difficulty in parenting abused children and there are no fixed and discrete groupings. To a certain extent, this makes a slight difference to the underlying picture. Another, perhaps more significant issue is that the survey was conducted at a fixed point in time and things do change. Had we completed this survey when Jemma was six or seven, we probably would have ended up in the middle group: coping, but with highs and lows. By the time she was 13, things were different and we would have definitely been among the third with very serious problems. The report is therefore representative of a changing population. Another reservation regarding the data, which the researchers point out, is that the return rate for the survey was only 34 per cent and was mainly from those parenting teenagers; hence those returning the survey were more likely to be the ones having problems. While this may be true, I believe it is also the case that many of the adopters experiencing very significant problems would not have had the time and energy to complete and return it, potentially skewing the data in the opposite direction.

Despite these possible limitations, this report provides significant evidence regarding the nature of adoption and the outcomes. It is clearly at odds with the picture often painted in the media and by some adoption groups, and also clashes with the expectations one could assume to be true based on current government agendas. In its defence, the government has taken note of the situation, and initiatives such as the Adoption Support Fund are intended to address some of the problems, in addition to the other measures outlined in *Adoption: a vision for change.*

In terms of the versions of events that are reported and made available to prospective adopters, I believe the facts have often been glossed over or understated. Although the effects of abuse on children and the probable issues that result are clearly outlined to adopters, the potential long-term effects on their lives have not been. Current adopters who are experiencing 'highs and lows' in their placement are called on to speak at preparation groups, but those of us who have weathered very severe problems are generally not invited. We are anonymous, despite making up about a third of adopters, and the fact that an unhappy outcome is statistically just as likely as a really happy one is not generally promoted. It is perhaps here that the vulnerability of prospective adopters, whose aspirations and needs are largely driven by an emotional yearning, comes to the fore. Under such circumstances, positivity and hope can easily outweigh caution and any thought of failure.

In the autumn following Jemma's 15th birthday, she went missing. We knew her usual haunts and, with the help of friends, soon found her and brought her home. She then absconded from school and the police picked her up walking along the edge of a dual carriageway. On a third occasion, a member of the public reported her to be randomly knocking on doors in an area of town known to be linked to her birth family and asking if her birth mum lived there. She was also making quite serious threats to harm us. This continued for more than a week, and an urgent multidisciplinary team meeting was called at which it was decided that Jemma needed some time away from the situation, the theory being that she had been overwhelmed by the effects of therapy and her increasing awareness. The thing that was finally bringing Jemma closer to us had also brought up some very confusing, unrecognisable and frightening feelings for her about her identity and place in the world, and this must have been a bewildering time for her.

Jemma's social worker arranged for a brief period of respite care and asked us to deliver her to the local office with a bag containing what she would need for three or four days away. I was in a state of total turmoil, wanting her to both stay and go, for different reasons. There was a large part of me that knew we were all at the end of our tether and needed this time apart. Hopefully, then, we could patch things up again and move on.

We packed her bag and dropped her off. She would not speak to us and, after we'd made a few attempts to say goodbye, the social worker advised us to leave. We didn't know where they were taking her but were told they would let us know. It felt like they just whisked her away. Sadly, she has not lived at home with us since.

When we adopted Jemma, this outcome was not even vaguely on our minds. Unfortunately, this sequence of events, or ones very much like them, is not that uncommon for those families in the 'final third'. Many of their children leave home early and traumatically, despite what some experts say about this only happening in three per cent of adoptions. The terminology and recording of such outcomes are variable and confusing, and conceal an important truth.

The term 'disruption' has generally been applied to adoptions that have broken down to the point that the child has been removed or, in the case of older children, has walked away and been returned to the care system. That seems like a straightforward definition until you take into account that different groups have chosen to apply limitations on this simple concept. In our case, as in many others, the local authority chose not to count our adoption breakdown as a disruption under their definition. Mostly, it seems, local authorities apply that term only when the child is returned to care before any adoption order is made, or very shortly after. Thus, it might be true to say that the 'pre-order disruption' rate is three per cent, which as far as I can work out would be a reasonable and true statement. But if you look more widely, at the disruption figures for children who have been in placement for some years, the results become more unreliable as time passes, because long-term records are not maintained and different parties choose different interpretations of the term 'disruption'.

Selwyn and colleagues (2014) point out that it is virtually impossible from the data currently available to derive an accurate 'post-order' disruption rate. They say it is more likely to be between two and nine per cent.

Previous studies (for example, Selwyn et al, 2006; Rushton & Dance, 2006) have indicated overall disruption rates of about 20 per cent and, as far back as 1998, Lowe and colleagues drew attention to the absence of disruption rates in the official statistics. Yet, more than 20 years later, these numbers are still not recorded and collated.

In yet another study, John Randall (2013) studied all the placements in the voluntary adoption agency in which he was working over a whole decade. Between 2001 and 2011, Families for Children placed just over 300 children. Randall defined disruption as being any placement that terminated before the child reached the age of 18 and found that 3.8 per cent of adoptions disrupted pre-order and a further 3.7 per cent post-order. He acknowledged that the post-order group might be underestimated as he could not trace all of them, and that there could also have been further disruptions in the sample group before all of them reached 18 (some were only in the early years of their adoption during the study period). So he found the overall disruption rate to be at least 7.5 per cent, and very probably higher.

Although this sample group was relatively small, it seems to be complete, and Randall's qualification of his data and their limitations is clear. His numbers support the general finding in the 2014 Selwyn study.

I am therefore perplexed that those using statistics as a crude measure of success and failure continue to promote the magic figure of three per cent as a rate of disruption, their implication surely being that 97 per cent of adoptions are successful. I am sure any prospective adopter would gladly latch on to this figure without question. I believe that interpreting the crude figures in this way does nothing to serve the cause of adopters. Even if this figure were true, placements that are in severe difficulty but do not disrupt do not provide any guarantee of quality, as Randall points out. There is rarely a full exploration of what this can mean to the lives of adopters and that they might consider the adoption to have broken down, even if the child remained at home until 18.

When the issue of adoption disruption was investigated in 2017 by the BBC Radio 4 programme *File on Four*, there were some startling revelations. Although its investigation comprised a survey, not a scientific study, it did feature nearly 3,000 respondents, which in terms of sample size beats any previous research by miles. Only 27 per cent said they found adoption to be 'fulfilling and stable'; 45 per cent found it 'challenging but stable' and 63 per cent said their child had been aggressive towards them. Around a third thought they hadn't been provided with enough information about their child before they adopted.

The research by Selwyn and colleagues and by Randall also went deeper than searching out crude data; their underlying objectives were to find the factors that affected the success of adoptions and suggest what could be done to predict failure and, potentially, head it off. Their number-gathering and statistical analysis were merely a part of this exercise and, although the data are compelling, as an adopter in search of a definition of success or failure, I do not believe that numbers alone can ever tell the full story.

Adoption agencies find 'families for children, not children for families', and most adopters will be conversant with that phrase, along with the one that offers children 'a forever mummy and daddy'. When I came to adoption, that's what I wanted to be – a forever daddy. I think this is an unconscious expectation of any parent: I don't believe there are many people who plan parenthood as a temporary measure, and adoption is no different. When we started out, I did not have in mind that Jemma would leave as she did or that our relationship would be so fraught and difficult, or, for that matter, that I would be abused by her.

I realise that horrible things happen in a lot of families, things do not always work out and that children leave home early and have poor relationships with their birth parents too. However, I suggest that, for adopters, there is a different dimension that sets us apart. Birth parents do not have to be assessed before they are allowed to become pregnant, do not have to be matched with their offspring by a third party, are even allowed to smack their child if they wish (not that I am condoning that) and, most importantly, do not come to parenthood from a position of acute loss. This final point is not true for all adopters, but it is for most of them, and many have previously endured years of involuntary childlessness, disappointment and hurt. This sets up a raft of feelings and expectations that non-adopters do not have about their children, and attaches an added element to the concept of failure.

Naïvely, I did expect to have a child whom I could love, and who would love me back and continue on good terms with me as their parent well into their adult years. I didn't even think about this; I assumed it was bound to happen. I was not so naïve as to expect there would be no problems or discord whatsoever, but I expected this to be minimal and resolvable, and to make us stronger in the long run. I wanted us to carry on growing together as a family, far into the future, in the way that I see most other families do. I would like to think that this was what Jemma really wanted too. And then, after only 13 years, she was gone. Based on this most fundamental measure of success, I consider that, regrettably, our adoption failed.

It seems ironic that, although I find it hard to avoid this conclusion, from the perspective of the government, the local authority and many others on the outside of our adoption, it would be considered a success. The placing agency would have received its inter-agency fee, the local authority had moved a child out of the care system (for most of her childhood at least) and, statistically, we did not show up as a disruption because of the local authority's interpretation of that term. Hence, we could be seen as one of the 97 per cent of adoptions that did not break down. Unfortunately, these are the objective and measurable factors that are used to validate the adoption agenda.

For me as an adopter and a dad, and based on my own subjective and qualitative measures, the term 'breakdown' cannot be defined simply by looking at a child's place of residence. I consider that our adoption broke down in many ways long before Jemma left us, and my experience of being her parent did not match the picture I had in my head when we set out. I had wanted to have a family, like anyone else, and for that family to look and behave and feel like a 'normal' family.

What is 'normal'? As far as I am aware, not many of my neighbours, friends and associates have had children who attacked them, verbally abused them and threatened them throughout their growing up. And none of them has followed their child around the country from children's home to children's home during their teenage years. That is what we ended up doing. The respite care Jemma was sent to when she left us was 120 miles away, allegedly the only placement available at such short notice. When we finally got to visit her there, we found the home, although very clean on the inside, was sterile in appearance and situated in a poor part of town. There were shuttered-up properties close by, and an industrial estate. Broken glass and other debris littered the road outside. Over the next three years, we were to follow Jemma around the country to numerous equally dismal destinations, while the local authority argued their case in court that we were unfit to be her parents.

She was moved three times in the first year alone, re-enacting some of the trauma of her early life, and we watched her behaviour deteriorate. If anyone was acting as an unfit parent in all of this, it was the local authority. Things only became more settled when the court became actively involved and ordered that a suitable placement be found. During these years, we learned to parent Jemma 'at a distance' and spent most weekends either visiting her or collecting her to bring her home for a few days. This was hard work, very tiring and often demoralising, as the staff at some units treated us as perpetrators and seemed set on splitting us from her. Despite this we persisted, like many of the parents Selwyn and colleagues describe in their study, and Jemma continued to want to have contact with us and then wanted to return home permanently. I am not sure if and how we could have coped with this because her behaviour had worsened and we were only just managing short periods with her. Jemma returning home permanently would have presented some serious challenges. It had become virtually impossible anyway, because by this stage the local authority seemed hell-bent on obtaining a care order and legally deleting us as her parents.

It is perhaps the bitterest irony of all that the same body who encouraged us, assessed us and approved us to become adopters then attacked us for failing. It is also perplexing that they were doing this while, on paper at least, we still met most of the government definitions of success. If they won their application for a care order, Jemma would simply be recorded as yet another child being taken into care and we *still* would show in the statistics as one of the 97 per cent of adoptions that, allegedly, do not break down.

There are no national qualitative or detailed data with which to view the long-term impact of adoption and make comparisons over time. Even if there were, as I said at the beginning of this chapter, measuring success in adoption still depends on who you are and where you stand in relation to it, and there would probably remain great disparity in how any findings were viewed. I think some of this can be explained by understanding the difference in how those inside and those outside it perceive the nature of adoption. From the inside, I see my role of adoptive parent as a very personal, life-changing, human experience; from the government's outsider perspective, my role is to be a resource – agencies 'find families for children'. To put it bluntly, they recruited me to do a job. My own experience of adoption was not taken into consideration – all that mattered was the placement of the child.

This mismatch in objectives is not obvious at first and doesn't get tested if a child settles well into an adoptive placement, with few problems, but for those of us with severely challenging children it can soon become apparent.

Many adopters have written about their lives, the trials and tribulations adoption brought them, the joys and heartaches. Some have added to the published work of professionals (or perhaps it is the other way around?), and between them they have provided a raft of strategies and helpful advice, from both the inside and outside of adoption, on how to be a successful adoptive parent. Having read quite a few, I've noticed that those by adopters seem largely to be written by parents who would fit in to the middle category of the Selwyn study – those experiencing highs and lows, but mainly highs. These are generally encouraging, positive and aspirational books that I know many adopters find really helpful. The message I get from some of them is, 'Here is a way to do adoption that will make it work.' As an adopter who couldn't make it work, no matter what I tried, unfortunately I also get another message, a negative one, one that says, 'If only I'd been better informed, more switched on and more responsive to my child's needs, things could have been different. If only I'd been a better dad.'

I know this is my message, my hang-up, my stuff but, nonetheless, this reassuring focus on adoptive life as a noble and ultimately rewarding enterprise seems to be pervasive in the literature. This is the image promoted as the face of adoption. The question this raises in me is: 'Everyone else seems to be joyfully finding success amongst the chaos, so why can't I?'

I know this is not the case, that the picture presented is flawed and many of us are not finding joy and success, as is proved by the data. However, it is not only the government and professionals who seem to be giving out this very limited and optimistic view of adoption. A number of adopters also seem to be promoting this picture, so why is that? I believe there are very good reasons why this version of events is usually the one that gets pushed to the front of the adoption stage.

Adopters with children who are relatively easy to parent have departed stage-left at the earliest opportunity and are getting on with their lives. Those of us with exceedingly difficult children, poor and inappropriate support and all sorts of resultant problems, are stuck backstage, trying to make sense of all the props. We feel that we should be on next but we daren't go out there with the kids still looking like this, and now there's smoke coming from the costume store and some little darling has suspended the box-office cat by its tail from the lighting gantry and we need to get it down. We are very much out of sight and unable to make ourselves heard, other than with the occasional scream of frustration.

Meanwhile, those on stage are predominantly in Selwyn's middle grouping, who may have struggled initially but are making a decent life of it. These parents have had some notable success, their child seems settled and now they have the time and energy to 'put something back' and are joining in the mission of the adoption professionals to tell the rest of us how it's done. It is a worthwhile cause, but what they report is what was acted out in their adoption and how they dealt with it successfully. It is their reality. This forms a major part of what the audience sees and goes on to understand as the rewarding and transformational power of adoption. This is how to do it and get it right.

I am not oblivious to the irony in all of this. Like my fellow adopters who probably had a better experience of adoption than I did, I am writing this book from the perspective of my own experience. It is partly an expression of my own personal struggle. It is certainly not my intention to take a cynical snipe at the views of others, because I genuinely believe they are adding to the pool of helpful and supportive resources available to adopters. I wish this had all been available when we applied to adopt. However, the fact remains that a large minority of adopters do not recognise this positive version of adoption and its implied measures of success. It is not their reality. What's more, if I am one of this 'unsuccessful' minority, and I get hooked into these messages and the inherent projections they carry, it can be detrimental.

If, for example, someone comes to adoption from the trauma and loss of infertility, with a consequent residue of self-doubt, only to be confronted with a very angry child who seems to hate him and for whom he can apparently get nothing right, this can present him with an intense emotional challenge. On top of that, he doesn't get good support from his local services and, if anything, feels blamed and criticised. This is not what he thought he was signing up for. Apparently, he can't do it as well as everyone else does; no matter how much he reads, learns, attends classes, uses strategies, tries to be the perfect dad, it just gets worse. What then? Why is he such a failure?

At this point, I want to shout STOP! I want to tell this adopter: 'What you are basing many of your thoughts, actions and beliefs on is probably not realistic, not true and certainly not healthy, for you or for those around you.'

A difficult adoption can take over your life. It can't be 'fixed' and is never perfect. We may battle and endure but, try as we might, things just get worse and spiral downwards as we push the bar of what we tolerate ever upwards, and normalise what has become a very abnormal way of living. I believe that this is something into which lots of us who were placed with severely damaged children unintentionally slip, and then find hard to escape from, and it seldom turns out to be a success story by many adopter measures.

I have been a victim of this. I dedicated so much to trying to make our virtually impossible adoption work to some idealised stereotype that I lost track of all other aspects of my life: my relationships, friends, interests and, finally, my self. I became a different person. I believe that being an adopter diminished me at times and was extremely unhealthy.

One experienced adopter told me recently about her story and feelings of loss, having parented a very troubled child over many years. In her view, 'They sold me a dream, and handed me a nightmare.' I know what she meant but, while my own subjective assessment is the one that influences me most, the views of others do matter to me, even when they seem at odds with my own.

Well-meaning friends still say how lucky Jemma is to have us as her parents and to have had the childhood she did. Understandably, they are looking at things purely from the point of view of success for Jemma. From that perspective it's not all bad, and their argument is not totally lost on me. I think it would be irrational for me to discount some notable successes for Jemma that resulted from our adoption, regardless of how I feel about its impact on me personally.

She learned to read and write, for one thing, which may seem basic but, had we not intervened, she could have ended up unable to do either very well. She is able to show concern for others, despite her erratic behaviour and unpredictable temperament. She developed skills in music and sport, and she understands how to behave in a variety of settings, even if her emotional instability sometimes gets in the way of this. Most of all, she knows right from wrong; she is often remorseful when she has done something to hurt someone. All these qualities, and more besides, were at the very least enhanced because I am her dad and she is my daughter. I take pride and acknowledgement in that fact.

Also, so far as she is able, she knows that she is loved and cared about and, even though she will probably never come to trust us 100 per cent, she probably considers Anne and me to be the most important people in her life, and certainly the most constant.

On some level, we must have been partially successful in our original quest to become a family, and I suppose it would be easy from the outside to view our adoption as simply something that didn't quite work out as I had hoped, or that we were not suited to it, or I held too high an expectation of it. This assumption would be a mistake and would grossly underestimate my experience and its impact. It was profound. It has probably been the most significant and influential experience of my whole life, one that I would never have lived through, or even imagined, had I not become an adopter. I have been changed. It was not simply something that went wrong; it was highly traumatic.

Despite the enormity of it all and the time I have spent reflecting on this aspect of my life, I still find it hard to come to any clear and final conclusion about whether our adoption of Jemma was a success or a failure for me personally. I am not sure if this is because I remain very mindful of how those terms are generally used and what such notions might indicate, or if there is really any point to them in this context. I am also aware of my urge to discount any absolute conclusion that uses this language, as it is simply too hard to contemplate. I certainly feel far more comfortable with considering our adoption from the perspective of gains and losses. These are perhaps easier to talk about, and there have been many over the years. Not all of them might be obviously linked to the adoption: for example, I lost one career and gained a new one as a therapist; I lost several friends, and found some new, more dependable ones; I lost a way of looking at the world and gained a new understanding of myself and those around me. These are just a few of the consequences, none of which could have been predicted, and it is hard to balance the books and draw any conclusion about the sum of their impact on my life. However, sadly, I have to accept that I did not achieve what I initially set out to achieve in the way that I had hoped I would. I expected our family life to be fun and to last. If truth be known, when we started out I expected to be in that first third of adopters that Selwyn and colleagues describe in their study – the ones that have few or no problems and experience a life 'very similar to many other families in the community'. Perhaps I achieved some of it, in a roundabout and very unorthodox way, but the loss of that longed-for and somewhat idealised 'forever family' is one that will stay with me.

Thankfully the local authority was not successful in their court application for a care order and I remain officially Jemma's dad. Anne and I continue to parent her at a distance and when we speak with her of the past, her memories are generally those of a happy childhood. These recollections are not always completely accurate, as she also seems to have an idealised picture of adoption and of our life together, often remembering the good bits and pushing the more unpleasant aspects out of her conscious awareness. There are also regular periods when she reverts back to hating us and I know that, at these times, the version of events she relays to others is, conversely, not exactly rosy. However, out of all this mess, there has developed a bond and we all acknowledge, each in our very individual and peculiar ways, that we are a family.

When social workers, the local authority and the government speak of finding families for children, I question what image or model they have in mind. Do they picture a family like ours? Perhaps they hold no particular picture at all, just an ideal that children need parents and being part of a family can transform their lives. Whatever their motivation, they seem to focus on the immediate and not on the long term and, somewhat optimistically, on the effect of the placement on the child, rather than the potential consequences for the whole family. Hidden within this agenda seems to lie some hopeful belief that the needs of adopters are also being met and that the experience is a successful and virtuous passage for all. As someone living on the inside of adoption, I hope it is clear to any observer peering through this optimistic lens that many of us bobbing about in what seems to be the sea of success aren't waving but drowning.

References

Department for Education (2016a). *Adoption: a vision for change.* London: Department for Education. www.gov.uk/government/publications/adoption-a-vision-for-change (accessed 26 April 2018).

Department for Education (2016b). *Children and Social Work Bill. Impact assessments.* London: Department for Education. www.parliament.uk/documents/impact-assessments/IA16-008.pdf (accessed 26 April 2018).

File on Four (2017). *Adoption: families in crisis.* BBC Radio 4. www.listenersguide.org.uk/bbc/episode/?p=b006th08&e=b095rs05 (accessed 26 April 2018).

Lowe N, Murch M, Borkowski M, Weaver A, Beckford V, Thomas C (1998). *Supporting Adoption: reframing the approach.* London: BAAF.

Randall J (2013). Failing to settle: a decade of disruptions in a voluntary adoption agency in placements made between 2001 and 2011. *Adoption and Fostering 37*(2): 188–199.

Rushton A, Dance C (2006). The adoption of children from public care: a prospective study of outcome in adolescence. *Journal of American Academy of Child and Adolescent Psychiatry 45*(7): 877–883.

Selwyn J, Sturgess W, Quinton D, Baxter C (2006) *Costs and Outcomes of Non-infant Adoption.* London: BAAF.

Selwyn J, Wijedasa D, Meakings S (2014). *Beyond the Adoption Order: challenges, interventions and adoption disruption.* Bristol: University of Bristol. https://assets.publishing.service.gov.uk/government/uploads/system/uploads/attachment_data/file/301889/Final_Report_-_3rd_April_2014v2.pdf (accessed 26 April 2018).

Chapter 5
The trauma contagion

Trauma is like a nasty smell that follows you around; even though you can't see it or touch it, you just know it's there. It gets absorbed into the psyche and makes itself at home. The worse it is, the more avidly it clings. While it's very difficult to define it or put it into words, you can recognise its lingering aroma a mile off. Sometimes it seems to have drifted away but it can live on and affect its victims in a number of ways long afterwards. You never know when or how it might be triggered and sneak out for another assault on the senses, and what further damage it might cause. What is that smell?

Childhood trauma is no different. It follows adopted children into their new homes, wafts around them in their play, fills the air during tantrums and snuggles up to them at night. It is insidious, deceptive and dangerous, and extremely hard to eradicate. It manifests itself in different ways and can replicate itself in a range of trauma-related experience in adoptive families. It is not something that arrives with the child simply as a disabling problem to be fixed. It is vital, it is living and it can go on to infect all those who come into contact with it.

As an adoptive parent, it took me some time – about 15 years to be precise – to recognise that I have been one of its casualties. I think I am still coming to terms with that fact, even though on some level I must have known it for some time. After all, I had seen Anne slowly being dragged down by the terror of it all over many years. I have seen her draw back when she finds herself in a kitchen with children where there are sharp knives lying about, and inexplicably in tears on many occasions. Despite all this, I think I had assumed my persona of being the 'strong' one was carrying me through, relatively unscathed. I was wrong.

Such a lot has been written about trauma and its many manifestations and effects. The term most often applied to the experience of trauma in adoptive families is vicarious or secondary trauma. This regards the child's trauma as primary and the impact of that trauma on those who come into close relationship with the child through adoption as secondary, or vicarious.

The same terms, vicarious or secondary trauma, are also used in counselling and psychotherapy to describe the impact of working empathically with clients suffering from the consequences of severe trauma. The therapist can inadvertently become affected by their client's experiences and current state of distress, and become distressed and traumatised themselves in the process. If this continues for some time and is not addressed by careful management and good clinical supervision, then it can lead to burnout or compassion fatigue. This phenomenon is not limited to psychology; most workers in the caring professions are vulnerable to the same problem.

As an adoptive parent, I have experienced the impact of my child's trauma and have learned that living with it changes life dramatically for everyone in the home. Having loved and cared for Jemma and been alongside her in therapy, I have been strongly affected by the dramatic influence her abusive early childhood had on her. I have found it upsetting and traumatising. I have also worked as a therapist and supervisor in a team supporting people suffering high levels of distress, many of whom have histories of childhood trauma, and here too I have often witnessed and been deeply affected by some of their suffering as I tried to engage with them on a deeply empathic level.

While the term 'vicarious' has been used to describe both affects, for me the quality of these two is very different and the definition does not fit well with my experience.

When working with clients, I follow my training. I use the techniques I have been taught and enlist the support I need from other professionals. An important part of this is my regular clinical supervision, which helps me to cope in the most demanding of emotional situations. Critically, at the end of the day, my clients are my clients and there it ends. I may hold them in mind periodically, but they are not my friends, I am not related to them in any way other than through our counselling relationship and I certainly don't take them home with me at night. My feelings towards them are restricted by the parameters of our limited working relationship. What I feel for them is real, but it is also contained.

The relationships I have with my children, on the other hand, are markedly different to my professional relationships and, while my empathic response to distress in my home and work settings may have some common features, qualitatively and effectively they are miles apart. For instance, I do not hold the same professional attitudes and boundaries towards my family as I do to clients. I do not love my clients as I do my family, and how their distress affects me and the meaning this has for me personally are very different. It does not surprise me that my triggers and responses to the trauma of my child are not the same as I experience with clients.

It is not just the emotional context that influences this disparity. I meet each client for an hour or two a week; I do not live with them. Being exposed to trauma vicariously on a 24/7 basis, in an inescapable and relatively uncontained environment, brings its own consequences. Living with it, rather than working with it, is a completely different ball game.

Nor does the term 'vicarious' adequately describe what happened to me as an adoptive parent: regarding my experience as purely secondary and putting it completely down to Jemma's trauma does not capture the full picture. It diminishes what has happened to me and it certainly does not do justice to what has happened to Anne, who, as the mother figure, took the brunt of Jemma's anger and aggression over many years. Being strangled, threatened with knives and hot irons, and pushed down the stairs are all traumatic experiences that could, of themselves, bring a person to therapy. That they are associated with or a consequence of contact with a person who was traumatised themselves in the first place makes no difference. Trauma is trauma.

On many occasions I had to stop Jemma from attacking Anne, sometimes taking a thump or two for my trouble. She would use knives and any other household implements that came to hand, so I became obsessive about putting things away. There were periods I dared not leave the two of them alone together and adapted my work hours to avoid it. It felt like we were living under siege.

These events increased in ferocity as Jemma grew older. Added to all of this was a daily barrage of threats, foul language, unreasonable demands and confrontation, which would under most circumstances be described as verbal and emotional abuse – this was the level of chaos and danger in which we lived.

I am in no doubt that what Anne and I experienced was primary trauma, which, in an adult-to-adult or adult-to-child setting, would come under the heading of domestic violence and abuse. It was separate from and different to the secondary trauma that came from our empathic response to Jemma's distress. Including it all under the general title of vicarious trauma shifts the focus onto Jemma's trauma and away from ours. I think this played a part in why it was largely overlooked or ignored by the professionals dealing with our case, as all eyes were on Jemma and her problems; any concerns regarding our safety and vulnerability came, predictably, way down the list. She was, after all, our child and our responsibility and there was an unspoken message that we needed to take charge and stop her doing this to us.

There was also a third facet to our adoption trauma. In the midst of all this mayhem, we tried to get help from anyone who would listen. Questions we had addressed during our gruelling adoption assessment process included how we would work with professionals – nothing was said at the time about some of them not wanting to work with us. Not all were competent or empathic and the system was quick to point the finger at us. A small number of workers were vindictive and, in a couple of instances, they were malevolent. The readiness of professionals to rapidly form a view and wield their power was very frightening, and some of what they wrote in reports about us and our parenting skills could have put them in court in a different situation. But within this culture we had little value and few rights, and that made me feel powerless and oppressed.

I want to stress that we also met many helpful, empathic and caring people who often worked beyond their brief in order to help us. We are still in touch with some of them, years later. However, my relationships with some professionals, their actions and treatment of me and the consequences for me as a father and human being were, frankly, extremely traumatising.

I have carefully considered whether naming these experiences as traumatic, in the true sense of the word, is valid. Some might say that they were just part of life's rich pageant, nothing too far out of the ordinary, and to be expected. It might have been confrontational and difficult to live through, but did it constitute trauma?

That view might hold water for some of what happened, especially in the early days. My expectations of the system were quite high and I know that the vast majority of professionals intend to do well, even when the system won't allow it. However, over time, my experience included such a mixed bag of events and interpersonal relationships that they have all become a disagreeable, dense fog in my mind. Some were good and others simply terrible, but I find that pulling them and their effects apart is not always easy. Looking at the various ways psychological trauma is defined helped me to begin to understand and shed some light on the question, how did what happened to me add up to trauma?

Trauma is derived from a Greek word literally meaning 'wound'. There are many definitions that sound very similar, mostly referring to emotional shocks and stressful events that have a lasting impact on the individual. Other terms include suffering, deep distress and severe emotional or mental distress caused by an experience. The general emphasis given in these definitions is on the lasting nature of trauma. Trauma changes people. Hence that becomes a key indicator of its occurrence: am I the same person afterwards as I was before?

Traumatic experiences can also have an effect, in addition to any affect. By this I mean that not only do people feel and think differently following trauma but there are often consequences for their future behaviour, development and wellbeing, so observing such effects in me could also provide evidence that I have been affected.

This offers me different avenues by which to consider not only the events as they occurred but also what they have done to me in the long term. Hence, applying two simple tests – does it fit with the definition and are the features of trauma present in me? – gave me a good insight into my differing experiences of seeking help from professionals.

There were many positive ones at first but, as time progressed and things became more difficult, these became less common and our relationships with some individuals became actively adversarial. These negative experiences were on a continuum that ranged from interactions that were simply annoying, frustrating or infuriating through to seriously traumatising events.

At the lowest end of this range we had to endure multiple meetings, frequently called or changed at a day's notice, that often resulted in no effective help. We were supposed to just drop everything and attend. The focus of these meetings could easily shift away from Jemma's needs and onto those of a particular service or department, or even onto a specific person at the meeting and their problems in providing a package of care. We would sometimes leave a meeting wondering who it had been for.

Then there were more serious encounters that were not only maddening but also insulting or blaming. These became more common as we became more stressed and worn down and the seriousness of the situation increased. For example, we were accused in one meeting of not engaging with social care and in another of not raising the issues soon enough for the help Jemma needed to be provided. The fact that we had unsuccessfully been banging on the locked doors of health and social care for almost 10 years was conveniently ignored.

Annoying and frustrating as all this was, I accept that this is part of everyday life and was not a source of trauma. It was exasperating for everyone, and most of the professionals involved seemed at times to be struggling against the very system they were a part of.

When Jemma finally left us and became enmeshed once again in the care system, things rapidly changed. Her social workers were free to dispute her diagnosis of attachment disorder, even though they were not qualified to do so. They found it easy to criticise the therapeutic parenting approach we had found worked for us, and even to question the approaches of the therapists involved with us at the time. This was ironic because social services had been the ones who commissioned and paid for this therapy, which was the best available. They talked about us 'holding her back' and being oppressive. We, allegedly, were the cause of the problem and not part of the solution. They produced highly critical reports that they told us about but would not let us see, some of which only came to light once our solicitor became involved. They contained many scathing opinions supported by clever distortions of the truth.

The power imbalance is so great in such a situation that if a professional wrote a report saying that the sky was yellow and I disputed this with written evidence that the sky was in fact blue, at most the report would be revised to say that 'the sky is yellow but allegedly, according to Mr Teasdale, it is blue'. This may seem farcical but all evidence is weighted so strongly in favour of professional groups that disputing a report's content is very difficult. Any assertion by us that what was being said was wrong could be totally ignored, no matter how we backed it up with evidence from our experience. As a result, factually incorrect information is scattered freely throughout Jemma's records and there is little we can do about it. Once written down by a professional, even the most erroneous and potentially dangerous information becomes fact.

I can vividly remember when the local authority applied for a care order and we first went to court. The grounds for the application were that 'the child is suffering or is likely to suffer significant harm and the harm, or likelihood of harm, is attributable to the care given to the child, or likely to be given to the child if the order were not made, not being what it would be reasonable to expect a parent to give to a child'.

Or, in plain English, Jemma was allegedly being harmed and our parenting was to blame. She needed to be removed from us to make her safe.

We had long fallen out with the education and social care authorities, due to what we saw as their inadequate response to Jemma's needs, and our strained relationship was reflected in the pages of a long court report outlining our misdemeanours, mostly comprising carefully selected and one-sided snippets of evidence, skewed interpretations and opinion.

I felt under attack, and in a way that I found quite devastating. I experienced their judgments and accusations as striking at a very sensitive part of my core beliefs – my beliefs about the importance of my family, who I am within my family and who I am as a person. I see myself ultimately as a good person and my children's protector, and certainly not as someone who would ever hurt them or any other child. Several local authority officers seemed to want to dispute and challenge those fundamental perceptions. I experienced this as an existential attack, which is probably why I found it so distressing. The person they were depicting and criticising was not the person I perceived myself to be.

The potential consequences were also very frightening: we faced never seeing Jemma again and we did not trust the local authority with her care. Anything could have happened to her. Anne and I both worked in jobs requiring enhanced Disclosure and Barring Service (DBS) checks, so our livelihoods were also at risk. We could both have lost not just our jobs but our whole careers. Thankfully Michael was an adult by this stage but there was also a potential for restrictions on our relationships with other children, if the local authority were believed. These were very powerful and intimidating threats that added to my already heightened anxiety and caused many sleepless nights.

Fortunately, we had an astute and extremely compassionate legal team who recognised the injustices. They supported us in so many ways, and not just through their advice and representation. Without them, I think I would have felt completely alone and even more vulnerable. I tried to keep firmly in mind the important fact that we did not make Jemma this way, others did; we were just doing our best to try to repair some of the damage and provide her with some hope.

After more than a year, the case came before a senior judge and the attempts by the local authority and various workers to discredit and harm us backfired. The care order was never granted and the judge criticised the local authority, but Jemma did not return home and there were other, subtler attempts to disrupt our relationship.

Some of the workers who had been caring for Jemma during this period had not even heard of attachment disorder, had no experience or understanding of adoption and seemed to believe that we were bad for her. In one placement, she kept a journal – something we had taught her to do as a useful outlet for some of her emotions. We noticed that this was being marked like a school book by the care workers and whenever she had written 'mum' or 'dad' it was crossed through and replaced by 'Anne' or 'Phil' and had a congratulatory star, a 'well done' or a smiley face next to it. I find it hard not to conclude that their actions were malicious. In another placement, the in-house clinician in charge of Jemma's care declared that Jemma would be better off developing relationships with professionals as she moved into adulthood, and not with us. Apart from this being a total insult to us as her parents, it made no practical sense, as the professionals in her life were extremely transient.

These are just minor examples of the many attacks that were made on our family, each adding to my stress and distress. Years later, Jemma apologised for some of the things she had said during this period but maintained that she was effectively coerced into colluding with the local authority agenda. We will never learn the whole truth and we had no real redress; complaints procedures are barricades masquerading as open doors – when we made a complaint about the lack of care and care planning Jemma had received, we were warned by one supposedly independent investigating officer that 'the more you push, the more they (the local authority) will push back'. He turned out to have longstanding relationships with the local authority.

Were all these events actually traumatic? Did they fit with the definition of trauma and did they traumatise me? In my view, they were, and I was (and remain) traumatised by them. They wounded me, caused great suffering and were severely distressing, even shocking at times. They have had a long-term impact and I have been changed by them. I am not the person I was before they occurred. I am more wary, cynical, anxious and angry. I used to believe that, although some workers were more competent and helpful than others, I could rely on the integrity and understanding of pretty much anyone who had chosen to pursue a career in the helping professions. I no longer hold this as a core belief and I now distrust professionals because I know that I cannot take competence, integrity and truth for granted. This continues to intrude into any new relationships I make with Jemma's current care team. There have been dozens of workers of many disciplines involved in her care in the last few years alone, and with each new team I feel my anxiety rising until I have had a chance to suss them out. While this may present as a safe and prudent way for me to behave, I don't think it is particularly healthy and it would not be my preferred way of being towards another person in any working relationship. I never used to be this way.

Ours is, regrettably, not an isolated case; I know of many adopters, through my personal and professional contacts, who have similar stories. The 2014 report, *Beyond the Adoption Order*, by Selwyn and colleagues also refers to this issue in less direct terms, particularly among the third of adopters experiencing severe difficulties. The report notes that 'battles' with services were common and parents were sometimes 'treated as though they were abusive' (Selwyn, Wijedasa & Meakings, 2014).

When I initially wrote about the effects of trauma on adoptive parents in the BACP journal *Therapy Today* (Collins, 2015), I was surprised by the response. The journal's circulation was, at that time, about 40,000 – practising counsellors and psychotherapists, mostly, spread widely across the country. I expected only a small minority of readers to be directly interested in this specialist topic. I received more than 30 direct replies, a significant number proportionately, mainly from adopters and foster carers who had similar tales to tell. Almost all recognised that they had been traumatised by their experiences of caring for an extremely damaged child, and that this trauma was not simply secondary. Many had experienced high levels of aggression and violence from their adopted child. Unhelpful and even hostile responses from services featured highly in their accounts, some were still in the midst of ongoing battles with the authorities and many described feeling threatened and undermined by the authorities' attitudes and actions.

The mechanisms that drive this harmful and dysfunctional dynamic are complicated and fuelled by cascading events, situations and interactions. While every family and situation is obviously unique, I think the sequence of what happens often looks like this.

- When a child is placed it may seem like the adopters and the professionals involved are starting in the same place, but they are not; they have very different agendas, expectations and needs. All is well when things go well but when they don't, these differences quickly become apparent. The more difficult the situation becomes, the more people get involved, often from outside the immediate adoption team.

- Adoption, attachment and developmental trauma are extremely complex. Professionals outside of adoption teams have surprisingly little knowledge of adoption and almost no understanding of the significance of trauma in the first two years of life. This is critical in how they respond to the situation. These professionals often make the assumption that the reasons for the child's behaviour lie outside the child and, by default, with the carers. The carers must be doing something wrong. This attitude is reflected in their safeguarding standpoint and does not take into account the child's background and history.

- The completely worn down and distressed adopters initially expect that services will have at least some answers, and services in turn willingly assume that expert position.

- When things worsen, the adopters' disappointed expectations and the lack of both understanding and resources within services create conflict, and working relationships spiral downwards. If the adopters challenge the services, their complaints are taken personally by some professionals and some allow this and their own issues to spill over into their work.

- Any joined-up thinking and co-operation that did exist evaporates. Managers protect their budgets and try not to commit to anything. Defensive communication, splitting, pairing and infighting ensue.

- By now, the adopters are fighting battles on two fronts. They probably fought to get services involved in the first place; now they are at war with some of the service providers and still need help with the child. They gradually lose faith and trust in the system, feel under attack and are traumatised further.

- Ultimately, rather than helping the adoptive placement succeed, services unwittingly add to the trauma and level of difficulty the family experiences. Everyone feels helpless and unfulfilled and, not wanting to hold those unpleasant feelings themselves, project them onto the other party in a variety of ways. At this point the group is totally dysfunctional.

While this is a very simplified version of what I have observed happening in my own life, I think this cascade of events, or ones very much like them, is a feature of many failing adoptions. Finding a way to stop or reverse this group process would require the many players involved to make a concerted effort to relate to one another in a different way and communicate at a much deeper level. While the same challenges would persist, this would at least provide a chance of dealing with them in a less destructive manner and in a way that would be far healthier for all those involved. Group dynamics are about relationship and I will explore this element of adoption in greater depth in the next chapter.

One consequence of being traumatised gradually, in different ways and over many years, was that I did not notice it for what it was. My response to any new challenge Jemma presented through her behaviour was simply to adapt, raise the bar and normalise what, to most people, was a wildly abnormal home life. My response to what I saw as the ineptitude and hostility of services was to get angry. There were peaks and troughs, which Anne and I survived only by strong teamwork and by help from the few remaining friends who had managed to stay after others had deserted. Even when they offered their support, we sometimes found it easier to politely refuse it because Jemma's behaviour was complicated, and small amounts of inexperienced help could ironically lead to yet another problem to sort out. We were so worn down by and locked into this intense struggle that everything outside of it paled into insignificance. And it was so hard to explain that it was difficult to believe anyone could possibly understand or help us. We became very isolated, both as a couple and individually, and laughter became as rare as dinner invitations. I couldn't find pleasure in anything we did and felt I had nothing to look forward to. The prospect of a solution from one of the many 'experts' we saw provided some hope but there were days when I sat on the stairs and cried when Jemma had left for school, and I could not work. Physical aches and pains were a common feature of my life and my GP diagnosed me with depression; the sick notes recorded 'stress at home'. Over time I acquired many of the hallmarks of trauma: anxiety, exhaustion, insomnia, tremors, edginess and feeling unable to cope. I woke each morning feeling dread: 'Am I still here?... What will today hold?'

I think the last year before Jemma left us was probably the lowest point of my life. It was suffocating.

The type of abuse we were subjected to by Jemma has had little recognition, even though it happens in a very significant number of adoptive families. It is as though it is a taboo subject and, where it happens, it is assumed to be the fault of the adopters. There was certainly no name given to it at the time.

Selwyn and colleagues' study was perhaps the first to report it formally. There is, as far as I am aware, still no significant research on the long-term effects of adoption-related trauma on adopters. There is, however, a new term now being applied to this type of abuse – child to parent violence (CPV). This is obviously not confined to adoptive families but it became the new big thing in adoption following the publication of the Selwyn research and strategies to deal with it. Even the government was prompted to provide grants to adoption support organisations to help them train staff to work with it. New experts emerged, who had 'done the training'. But these interventions, too, remain focused on the child and their needs. This work continues through an ongoing collaboration between AdoptionUK and PAC-UK (2018).

Regrettably, there is still no agreed definition of CPV, unlike, for example, domestic violence and abuse, and it is described in a variety of ways. Nor is there any consensus on how to manage it. The impact on adopters has largely been ignored or misunderstood and it remains a feature of the shadow side of adoption that only those directly affected by it fully understand. It has many facets and is not limited to vicarious trauma. This has been recognised by some adoption support workers but many still struggle to look beyond the trauma of the child when addressing the problems adoptive families face. In parts of the UK, foetal alcohol syndrome is still not recognised and understood as a problem, and it's likely CPV will also take a long time to drip through the system and become widely accepted.

When I attended Level 2 Safeguarding training in 2015, I asked the trainers about CPV and how they would deal with a situation where a parent was being physically attacked by their child. The two of them looked blank at first. When they did reply, their answers were based on three assumptions: that the parent must be a service user (ie. mentally ill); that the child needed safeguarding *from* the parents, as it must be the parents' fault; and that there was no real risk to the parents because, if the child is over the age of 10, they can call the police, and if the child is under the age of 10, they can easily physically restrain him or her. As one of the take-home messages of the day was 'Think the unthinkable', I found it disappointing that these trainers could not get their head around the fact that a child could be a perpetrator.

I knew nothing about trauma when we adopted Jemma, and if you had told me I would end up with my own trauma timeline as a result, I probably would have laughed at you. I can now recognise its foul odour in an instant. Thankfully, Anne and I no longer have to put up with Jemma's regular physical attacks as we now parent her from a distance and she is, technically at least, an adult. However, her physical absence has not stopped the trauma.

For much of the time, our relationship is fairly benign. Jemma rings us and sees us regularly, often asking for something that indicates she simply wants some attention. During these periods we are usually the best thing since sliced bread. Sometimes her contact with us is more manipulative and demanding, when she becomes verbally abusive. These may be times when she is feeling out of control herself and therefore needs to exert it over someone else; we are usually her first port of call. Every now and then she will feel the need to reject us in the most violent and extreme manner possible. This sometimes takes the form of allegations against us. Jemma has made many over the years, about many different people in her life, starting at school with relatively low-level accusations about teachers and increasing in seriousness as she got older. Initially they were about incidents involving physical or verbal abuse but once she became sexually aware, they often had a sexual content.

I have found these very difficult to deal with. The first ones levelled at me were very definitely traumatising. Being the subject of safeguarding and police investigations was frightening and distressing. Child abuse is one area of wrongdoing where innocence has to be proven, rather than guilt, and the prospect of the system 'getting it wrong' was very real. I experienced it as yet another attack on who I was and who I believed myself to be. Existentially, it was life-threatening.

Although the initial shock has passed and everything Jemma said was disproved even before she retracted it, its impact continues to haunt me. She has continued, periodically, to make allegations about past carers and professionals, and about Anne and me. I have now become used to these events and don't expect them to stop, but that doesn't mean they don't have an impact, rekindle old memories and raise my anxiety yet again. I can sense the horrible, churning feeling in my gut right now, simply as I think and write about them. I have been severely affected by them and have changed as a result.

In terms of their ongoing effects, I am cautious about taking on young female clients. I will also avoid situations where I am alone with children and young people who I don't know well. I was quite shocked when I first noticed this, as it seemed disproportionate and I used to love to be around children; it saddens me that my instinct now is to treat them like a threat. Most notably, I am careful never to be alone with Jemma again. There is too great a risk that she will later make allegations about me and my behaviour. I need to do this for my own safety, but it is a great loss to both of us.

I intend to remain a part of Jemma's life but I know she is both extremely vulnerable and extremely dangerous, so our relationship will always be boundaried by my need to stay safe. Above all, I cannot ever relax my guard: when, for the umpteenth time, I find myself pulled back into Jemma's drama triangle, I am dealing not just with her trauma responses, but with my own as well.

References

Collins D (2015). Living with your child's violence. *Therapy Today 26*(8): 22–26.

PAC-UK (2018). *PAC-UK & AUK Child to Parent Violence Project*.[Online.] PAC-UK. www.pac-uk.org/cpv/#CPV2 (accessed 26 April 2018).

Selwyn J, Wijedasa D, Meakings S (2014). *Beyond the Adoption Order: challenges, interventions and adoption disruption.* Bristol: University of Bristol. https://assets.publishing.service.gov.uk/government/uploads/system/uploads/attachment_data/file/301889/Final_Report_-_3rd_April_2014v2.pdf (accessed 26 April 2018).

Chapter 6
It's all in the relationship

It was a rainy Saturday morning when we pulled into the drive of Windingbrook House. I remember feeling quite calm and unaffected, although Anne was clearly anxious, if determined not to show it. The home's manager came out to greet us.

'Morning. How was your trip? Come on in.'

We followed her inside.

'How is she?' Anne asked.

'Obviously she's been a bit unsettled but she seems in a reasonably good mood today. I'll go and fetch her in a minute. Would you like a coffee?'

We sat ourselves down in the lounge and waited. The TV was on low in the background. We looked at one another and I had a slight touch of déjà vu; it was like the first time we ever saw Jemma, at her foster carer's, when she rushed into the room, looked at us and rushed out again. But today was totally different.

There had been few periods after Jemma left home when we went without seeing her for more than a couple of weeks. This was usually because of something minor we had allegedly said or done and, feeling hurt and rejected, she then rejected us temporarily. After a few days, we would usually get a phone call from her asking us to get her some item that she desperately needed, and how soon could we bring it to her? This was her way of reaching out and reconnecting. On this occasion the time gap had been much longer because she had made some serious allegations that I had sexually assaulted her. These needed to be investigated, and we had also needed some time to recover from the initial impact. The allegations had caused an unimaginable amount of upset.

After a few minutes, Jemma arrived with one of her care workers. Another girl staying at the home followed. Some quiet hellos were exchanged and Jemma sat on a sofa diagonally opposite us. The other girl wandered about for a minute or so, weighing up what was going on, and then was encouraged to leave.

'How have you been then?' Anne tentatively asked.

Jemma shrugged her shoulders, 'Okay.'

'What have you been up to?'

'Nothin' much.' Her voice lifted: 'I've gone back to college two days a week.'

'That's good, well done.'

Things went awkwardly quiet at this point. We all looked towards the TV for inspiration. After a minute or two, her care worker made some laughing remark about the programme we were not really watching and began to talk about a neighbour's dog that had managed to break through the fence the day before. The dog had been caught and order restored, much to the disappointment of the girls, who had wanted to keep it.

Other than saying hello, I hadn't said anything directly to Jemma up to this point and was quietly sipping my coffee. She sidled over and perched on the seat next to me.

'Would you like this? You can have it if you want.' She produced a creme egg from her pocket and offered it to me.

I smiled at her, said, 'Thank you Jemma, that's kind, I'll eat it later,' and took the egg.

A simple exchange, and yet these actions and the words that accompanied them were highly symbolic of our relationship. It was, in one fell swoop, an act of testing, of reparation and of reconciliation. These had been the main features of our relationship all the way along, and I believe her words were unconsciously quite deliberate. She didn't just offer me the egg, she asked me if I would accept it from her, and in saying yes, I was accepting her. This was her test of me and our relationship – was there still enough of it intact for us to build on it, repair it yet again, and be reconciled?

Following that day, we gradually resumed our father–daughter relationship. Much later, she retracted the allegations, but things were never to be the same. She had threatened and attacked Anne and me in many ways over the years and yet, perhaps bizarrely, I had seen this as part of her condition; I had got used to the pattern of threat, de-escalation, reparation and reconciliation. This time, it was different; the allegations hurt much more than the threats-with-knives. More than I can say. She really damaged me, and I don't believe I will ever fully trust her again. This is perhaps where the impersonal nature of her abuse became personal, and it changed our relationship irretrievably.

This adjustment was not a new phenomenon; things between us have changed in many ways over the years and no doubt, as in most relationships, they will continue to do so. Being in relationship is never a static process. Of course, there are also two sides to this and whatever I perceived our relationship to be is only my reality; Jemma will have her own view.

I find it hard to look back and plot the evolution of our relationship with any certainty, as my memory of some of what happened is pitted by the accompanying highly charged emotions, but I hope I can explain how it was for me in a way that makes sense.

There were many ways in which we bonded. Some of these were inevitable, given my caring role and the close proximity we had to one another over a long period. Even though things were pretty tense or even downright horrible during much of this time, we also had fun and did all the things other families do. There were birthdays and celebrations, walks in the park and times of great hilarity. Living through all this produced a connection with and a common understanding of one another. Simply being intimately associated with another person for a long while can do that. I loved her and cared for her, and that mutual affection was one of our bonds. I felt we had a kinship, over and above the one defined by the adoption certificate. We belonged to one another in a way that I felt was permanent. I had a definite sense from very early on in our relationship that I was her dad, and this was, perhaps, the connection that overrode whatever else went on between us.

I believe we also shared some unhealthy bonds, including those that resembled trauma bonds. The term trauma bonding was introduced by Patrick Carnes (1997), who noticed that in abusive and exploitative relationships the victim often bonds in a particular way to their abuser. These bonds are characterised by very intense and addictive feelings in the victim, who is repeatedly drawn back into the toxic relationship. I can recognise some of those qualities in our past relationship and in the harmful dynamic that was set up. Other aspects of our relationship played in this, not least my need to be Jemma's dad. A very astute and mindful counsellor friend of mine once remarked that whenever she saw me, she envisaged Jemma standing by my side. Emotionally I must have been carrying her around with me with such intensity that others could visualise her presence, even when she wasn't physically there. I don't think this was very healthy for me.

In terms of attachment, and drawing on the ideas of John Bowlby and Mary Ainsworth, it is clear that Jemma's attachment to me was not one that would be deemed to be secure; it was disorganised and ambivalent, as were all her attachments. However, the question of how *I* might be attached to *her* is less clear-cut. In its fundamental form, attachment is an enduring emotional bond that connects one person to another and that persists over space and time. To some degree I can relate to that, and again I am drawn back to my core belief that this is how a father relates to his child.

The conclusion I find this leads me to is quite startling. Birth parents are sometimes referred to as 'real parents', presumably based on the assumption that the biological link is the strongest and best (this can be quite insulting to adopters – if the birth parents are the real parents, what does that make adopters?).

Given all that has happened and my belief that I have now largely extricated myself from any trauma bond I shared with Jemma, I am left with the realisation that there is a part of me that can't let go of her completely and that will be forever 'Jemma's dad'. Surely this makes me her 'real dad'? This may be something that will take time to fully test and resolve.

Yes, I am attached to her, but I don't believe our relationship will ever be 'healthy' by most definitions. Being aware of my own trauma and the trauma bond that exists between us has helped me to move to a more settled, boundaried and safer position, but Jemma continues to be very vulnerable and very dangerous at times, and we remain in an abusive relationship where past traumas are repeated and new ones created. I can easily get drawn back into the drama triangle (Karpman, 1968), where I readily assume the position of rescuer or, less frequently these days, victim. I can't see that changing for the foreseeable future. Jemma is so out of sync with the world and so scared for much of the time that she desperately needs to be heard, seen and held by the people who love her most. I don't think I would ever get to a point where I would not be prepared to do that for her, so, from that perspective, my relationship with her is very much on her terms more than on mine.

When Anne and I first came to adoption, and before we knew anything about it, I assumed that any relationship I had with an adopted child would be slightly different to the one I had with our son, Michael, but fundamentally very similar. I expected it would be pretty normal in most respects. At the adoption preparation classes, we soon learned that the adopter–child relationship is complicated by the inescapable presence of the absent birth parent, and most notably the birth mother, who can continue to exert a significant influence on that relationship. This important facet of adoption was explained to us as the adoption triad, or the ABC of adoption – **A**dopter, **B**irth parent, **C**hild – which is usually drawn as a triangle, with one member of the triad at each corner, as drawn below:

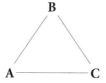

This was a relatively straightforward concept to understand in principle, but the day-to-day implications of it were not so clear until I experienced them. I can now see how this has worked out in our adoption and in the relationship we have shared. Jemma's birth mother, in particular, has been at times very large and very present in Jemma's thinking and emotional life, and this has obviously affected her relationship with Anne and me. In terms of thinking about adoption relationships from my adopter's perspective, however, I do not find this model is a complete or accurate representation of our involvement with one another.

For one thing, the way it is drawn seems to imply that all three participants in the triad are directly linked and of equal importance to one another. Personally, I don't find this to be the case. Although my relationship with Jemma has been greatly affected by her phantasy of an idealised birth mother, I have never actually met the woman. My link to her is purely via Jemma and the impact she has had, and will continue to have, on Jemma's life. To consider that we are directly related in some way through our adoption of Jemma seems to overplay whatever relationship we might have. Although this situation could theoretically change in the future, any relationship I have ever had with her as Jemma has grown up has been vicarious. We are not directly linked and to me the ABC of adoption is really an ACB:

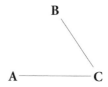

This focus on the adoption triad also ignores the impact of other relationships on our adoption. Here, I am referring mainly to those we have held with people in Professional groups, who, at times, have had more direct impact on our life together than Jemma's birth mother ever has. This changes the shape of things significantly:

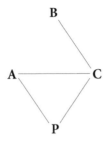

This open-diamond is a vastly simplified representation of the complex and compound relationships into which I entered as an adopter; there were of course other complicating elements, not least our son and our wider family, who also featured, and the many different people we encountered under that title of 'professional'. However, for me, it provides a helpful starting point from which to consider the principal relationships that significantly influenced my relationship with Jemma and the viability of our adopted life together. On a day-to-day basis, and especially when things deteriorated, it was the lower half of this open diamond that influenced whether the outcome was success or failure, and it is therefore worthy of some significant consideration.

Our relationships with professionals were not always good, and even some that started well degenerated over time. I referred in Chapters 3 and 5 to some of the difficulties Anne and I encountered with them and used the model of dynamic conservatism to consider how and why we had such problems. Ours was a common experience for adopters facing very significant challenges from our adopted children.

I have spent a lot of time wondering what made me so unlikeable to some professionals and what made them feel so hostile towards me. I have come to the conclusion that perhaps the key element driving this was to be found in the most basic of human emotions, most notably those of fear and anxiety and the avoidance of fear and anxiety, and the compensatory reactions of seeking some level of power and control.

As vulnerable human beings, our fears and anxieties are contained by a number of mental mechanisms that provide emotional protection of one kind or another, and every day we all use an assortment of these psychic defences in order to stay safe, or at least to stay feeling safe. At times we suppress emotions we don't want to deal with; we displace them onto other things; we smile when we are actually feeling sad; we laugh; we rationalise, and we project any unwanted feelings onto someone else. We all do this, and a whole lot more, in an unconscious attempt to maintain our emotional stability and feel generally okay within ourselves.

My wellbeing is largely dependent on this behaviour. If I become unable to hold onto a feeling of safety, I cannot function properly in the world, because my survival is key and takes precedence over everything else. Hence, I need to be able to contain my anxiety and feel safe in order to go to work, eat, sleep, look after myself and enjoy life. This emotional safety is basically the same feeling that Jemma finds so hard to hold on to and is mediated by the same psychological and physiological mechanisms I have described previously.

One thing that helps me to manage my stress levels in my daily dealings with other people is a tendency that I share with the rest of mankind: that is, I objectify others. This was clarified by the philosopher Martin Buber (2000/1923), who observed we have two options when we meet someone: either to meet that person in relationship or experience them as an object, and we can choose which position we take in every personal encounter. This provides two possible ways of relating: in an 'I–You' relationship *with* another person, or in an 'I–It' experience *of* them. I find it's not always that easy relating fully with everyone I meet because it takes thought, presence, determination and a good amount of emotional grit, so often I don't even try. I stay in my own little world, with my own thoughts and feelings, and make no real attempt to fully meet them in the here and now. It's almost as if there's not enough of me to do that in every encounter, and so I stay polite, superficial and slightly detached.

When individuals come together in groups, the same basic rules apply, but things become more complicated. Throughout the 1950s, psychoanalysts such as Elliott Jacques had been building on the work of Melanie Klein in considering how social structure, culture and function act as defence mechanisms in group situations, and how they affect the dynamics of organisations. Then, in 1960, Isabel Menzies Lyth published *Social Systems as a Defence Against Anxiety.*

Menzies Lyth studied nursing practices and, more specifically, the training of student nurses in a large London teaching hospital. She recognised that many of the ways of working in the hospital were organised so as to alleviate the anxiety of the nursing staff. This anxiety was to be found in the daily tasks of caring for ill people, some of whom would not recover, and in dealing with the expectations, anxieties and stress of both the patients and their relatives. The social system of the hospital had evolved to cope with this and defend against it, thus helping the staff 'to avoid the conscious experience of anxiety, guilt, doubt and uncertainty'.

This defensive action took many forms. The nurse-patient relationship was split by breaking down the workload into discrete tasks, and so each nurse was protected from having contact with any one patient throughout the totality of their illness; people became depersonalised as 'patients' or 'cases', and nurses were encouraged to detach themselves from and deny any feelings towards them. Some functions were impaired and things didn't get done as staff tried not to make decisions and found various ways to shrug off responsibility. Lyth also talked about staff 'clinging to the familiar' and avoiding change, which then only happened at points of crisis.

Decades later, the same work practices persist. Just recently, a family friend noted that, during her entire pregnancy, she never saw the same midwife twice, and anyone who has been an inpatient will have noticed the number of shifts and staff changes that take place each day and how the emphasis is on tasks and routines. As essential as these are, they do offer a mechanism by which patients and staff avoid really getting to know one another, despite the intimacy of the situation. I recognise similar practices when I work with an acute community mental health team. We meet very distressed, chaotic and sometimes dangerous people, many of whom are at a high risk of harm to themselves or to others. To reduce the anxiety associated with this, we hide behind a raft of defence mechanisms similar to the ones Lyth reported. As an organisation, the relationships we have with our clients are mediated by numerous policies and procedures and hindered by the fear of consequences. Many of the decisions we make have the group's self-interest at heart, rather than the interests of clients, as we protect ourselves from the risks associated with poor outcomes.

This anxious and defended behaviour is not restricted to medicine. Similar traits are found in the social systems of most caring professions and, as our home situation worsened and Jemma needed more help, these played a major part in my increasingly strained and confrontational relationships with some professionals. The language used when talking about these relationships is often very revealing of what is going on beneath the surface.

Each person who initially came to help us soon took on a title and mantle, such as 'social worker'. Later they might be a 'professional', who discussed our case with other 'professionals', and finally a 'service provider'. At each stage, I experienced a subtle change in our relationship.

Once a 'service' is being provided to a 'service user', this immediately creates not just a separation between two individuals but a hierarchy of status: one holds power over the other by virtue of being in a position to provide (or withhold) something they need.

These same principles apply in all helping professions, even though they may have their own specialised vocabulary of titles and terminology. Any provider holds all the cards in this game, and different names, roles and identities can be used to maintain that power and control and maintain the distance that allows them to manage their anxiety.

Relational dimensions of helping and being helped

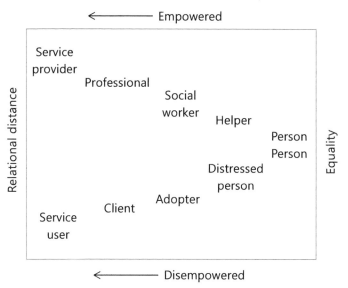

The relational distance these terms create is part of the objectification of others to which Buber alludes. When I translate the help I offer to another human being into the provision of a service, I increase the likelihood of missing that opportunity to fully relate to them. I am more likely to experience them as an 'it' or an object than I am to meet them as a real person in a meaningful relational encounter. The by-product of this is that it helps me to avoid some of the stress and anxiety I may be feeling, which would only be increased if I were to get to know them as a vital, hurting, vulnerable and distressed person.

I recognise this language in my work in mental health services, where it is the norm to think of the people we serve as patients and service users. It is not uncommon to hear a professional pronouncing of a client: 'His problems are all drink-related' or, 'Her behaviour is all down to her personality'. There is no malice intended in this but it obliterates the alternative view: that the alcohol-dependent man is drinking in order to self-medicate, and the distressed woman's behaviour is her only way of communicating the distress of her abusive childhood. To me, these interpretations and use of distancing language point to an avoidance of a harsh truth: that many of the people we meet and the situations they are in are beyond our help or understanding. All we can do, in some cases, is simply patch them up and send them back to the trenches. It provokes less anxiety to depersonalise the patient and point to their failings than to accept that a situation is hopeless. Unfortunately, this self-preservation also limits the effectiveness of our individual human encounters.

As a distressed and worn-down adoptive parent, I wanted to be seen, listened to and recognised as an individual person in a unique set of circumstances, not as a 'service user'. I needed to feel validated, respected and cared for, and I expected to receive this when I turned to others for help.

My relationships with professionals were tested further because I also had a very definite sense that I did not, unilaterally, create the circumstances that placed me in the position of needing help. I did not make Jemma this way, others did; services played a very clear and major part in the adoption and what went on before it. I believed I was entitled to expect their help in resolving some of the mess that resulted and that they had passed on to me, albeit I was a willing volunteer.

Moreover, the education, health and social care professionals always took the expert position in all of their dealings with us. Initially I assumed they knew what they were on about and, indeed, were experts on my world, but even when I realised this was not so, it was still the case that they were being paid to provide me with support. I was therefore entitled to have expectations of them – namely, that they would be effective in some form or another in providing the help I needed.

And finally, when our adoption was clearly in trouble and we sought help, I expected that we would all sing from the same hymn sheet. I naïvely mistook the same tune for the same song, but when it came down to it, the professionals were not singing the same lyrics as me. My objectives and measures of success were significantly different to theirs (see Chapter 4) and what subsequently happened may still have fitted many of their criteria but it was not what I had in mind.

Thus, a clear gap emerged between the professionals and me that widened every time it was tested. This was the start of a cycle of deteriorating relationships and the cascade of events I described in Chapter 5 and which I will elaborate upon here, using some of the models I have discussed in this book. This view is based on feedback from several professionals with whom we maintained a good relationship throughout our problems, and on my own personal experience.

The practitioners dealing with us in the early stages knew us pretty well; we already had a relationship with them and I felt they met with us on a very personal level. They knew our history and the difficulties we were in, and I believe they recognised our anxiety and vulnerability and tried their best to help us and to alleviate this. Our involvement with one another was relational and often subjective in the 'I–You' sense. I still felt valued and validated as a human being, and managed to contain any frustration I had with the way things were going and the ineffectiveness of the system. I imagine I was seen as doing my best in a difficult situation and came across as simply being in need of help and grateful and responsive towards anyone who offered it.

As the situation worsened and the level of difficulty grew, the technology of their social system (the methods and techniques they used) became inadequate to deal with it, and they ran out of ideas. Although these workers held on for a while to their theory about who they were and what they were supposed to be doing (their values and beliefs), eventually the structure of the system (their rules, procedures and policies) drew them to involve a wider group of professionals in the hope of finding a solution, and possibly helped contain their own anxiety in the process by spreading the burden of responsibility. Unfortunately, these new people did not know us or our history and had extremely limited experience in the specialist field of adoption. We were rapidly relegated to the status of 'service user'.

At this stage, we were extremely worn down and would have accepted help from an intergalactic being with two heads if they offered something that looked like it might make a difference. The grateful, jovial, easy-going adopter had been replaced by a frazzled, sad, angry one, and my relationships with some of the key professionals involved took a sharp downward turn.

My expectations were that they would not only be competent and effective but that they would also be able to both regulate their own emotions and leave their personal issues at home. I did not expect to have to make allowances for their bad day, bad mood or even bad marriage, and yet at times this is what I found myself doing, as the personal issues of some professionals made themselves very evident in our regular meetings.

I certainly was not prepared for their reaction to my simply saying how I was feeling, which aroused an astonishing level of anger and vindictiveness. One senior practitioner informed me that he believed some workers felt professionally threatened by me, and that this explained their response to what I thought was my being transparent and genuine with my feelings.

Many of the workers who were dealing with us were quite used to clients knocking over chairs and being openly aggressive. In those circumstances, it was probably easy for them to take the high moral ground and apply the defences of the system to full effect. I managed to refrain from physical and verbal aggression and maintained what I considered to be a generally respectful and reasonable stance. I was, however, at a low ebb both physically and emotionally, and I pulled no punches when it came to explaining how the impersonal nature of being a service user affected me and how the countless meetings were actually changing nothing. Being on the receiving end of carefully composed emails laden with highly emotional content that was also factually accurate and incisive and drew attention to the ineffectiveness of the system was possibly harder to defend against than the occasional flying chair and angry insults. Being faced with the raw-yet-controlled emotion of an unappreciative and angry service user must have been quite invalidating and may well have produced an existential anxiety in some individuals. I was also challenging the culture and effectiveness of their social system in a way that they found hard to ignore, which was their preferred way of dealing with difficult situations they couldn't make go away.

This is why, I believe, my attempts to communicate in this way were repelled at all levels and why, whenever I voiced any dissatisfaction or challenged services, it was construed as an unreasonable attack. They responded with some considerable hostility, which was often passive and manipulative. For instance, when I challenged the fact that it took our attendance at four meetings to arrange two evenings of babysitting, it was recorded in a report that we 'would not engage fully with services in providing us with respite care'. When I criticised the totally inappropriate response of the education department in the presence of a teacher, she burst into tears and curled up in a ball as if mortally wounded. The rest of that meeting was consumed with her welfare and needs, and I came away wondering whom it had been for and sensing that I had been placed in the role of perpetrator.

In a nutshell, much of what I did and said was meant as a way to try to engage in a frank, meaningful and relational dialogue in order to get the best for Jemma, but instead it raised such high levels of anxiety and feelings of failure in some workers that they felt driven to defend themselves against the danger they perceived. As I see it, their final throw was when Jemma finally left home, and they seized the opportunity to project it all back onto Anne and me in the form of a care order application. I had lost my prior status as a vulnerable, hurting, distressed person in need of help, and had lost my faith in them as competent and caring helpers. They had started seeing me as an ungrateful and difficult service user who needed to be brought to book, and I stopped seeing them as human beings.

At about this time, I wrote in my journal:

> I think I am also cross with myself because I no longer see them as people. I am worn out and if I had the choice I would simply cut all ties with the lot of them. To never have to speak to any of them ever again would be a relief and would help preserve my sense of self. Unfortunately, I have to maintain some contact with them because Jemma needs the services they represent. I am looking forward to the day we can simply walk away but for now, and as long as she needs services, I am stuck with them.

This sentiment is echoed throughout the pages of my journal, which regularly recorded my frustration, anger and sadness. That said, not all of my experiences with professionals were bad. We had some really good, equal, productive and highly supportive relationships too. The problem was that the workers who were adept at regulating their emotions and not bringing personal baggage into meetings, and who were skilled at staying both professional and human even in the presence of significant tension and anxiety, were often overruled by those who weren't. The power imbalance is often so great in these circumstances that just one defended, hostile and resentful professional in a key position can hold sway over the whole group.

This often had its own consequences, as it triggered the next step in the cascade: the splitting and pairing and infighting between agencies and departments, and the taking of sides. Sometimes the splits were obvious; sometimes they were hidden. Occasionally, representatives of different agencies would agree with us in private on what Jemma needed but find it impossible to achieve it in the wider group. To say they did not all get on with one another would be an understatement.

The blunt instrument that was usually to be found lying in the corner of any meeting room was the issue of funding. This could be retrieved at any point and used to create an impasse between services while they argued about who was paying for what. Sometimes it was used as a delaying tactic; nothing happened, and eventually whatever decision was being avoided became superfluous and could be forgotten. This served the purpose of the system but did nothing for Jemma and added to my frustration because, frankly, I didn't care who was paying; I just wanted the professionals to sort it out like adults and not to be continually playing pass-the-parcel with us. I did often wonder what amazing things could be done if all the energy and resources that were being put into not providing a service were simply channelled into helping us instead.

The gradual deterioration in Jemma's behaviour, and in my relationship with her, paralleled the deterioration of relationships in the group. Service providers often added to the trauma and difficulties we experienced as a family, rather than helping our adoption succeed. As enemies and allies manoeuvred around the battlefield of our multidisciplinary team meetings, mutual trust and respect was markedly absent. This dynamic gave rise to a lot of defensive behaviour as new threats were anticipated and dealt with.

It had been relatively easy to slip over the edge and into this cascade of increasingly negative encounters and to end up in a dysfunctional heap at the bottom. The psychologist Jack R Gibb (1961) considered communication to be key in changing this type of interaction in small groups. He noted that 'one way to understand communication is to view it as a people process rather than a language process' and therefore look at it in behavioural terms. Interestingly, this is not unlike the way we had learned to interpret Jemma's behaviour as a language; it was only when we started doing this that we began to get an idea of what was going on for her. Her behaviour was, at times, the only way she could communicate her internal turmoil. Unfortunately, it took me a while to recognise that a parallel process was occurring within our group meetings.

In our multidisciplinary group meetings, the behaviours that predominated could be categorised as evaluation, control and superiority, and these regularly won out over their more supportive behavioural counterparts of description, non-directive openness and equality. This produced a pattern of circular responses that, once established, became self-generating. To stop it, one party would have had to take the conscious decision to move away from it. Unfortunately, none of us did, and the dynamic stopped the group functioning and prevented it from reaching effective solutions.

I find it hard to believe that anyone who was part of that changing group over the months and years gained much satisfaction from it, or actually came away from it feeling they had done a good job. Objectively, there were no good outcomes for Jemma and she was often invisible amid the shenanigans that doubled as process and procedure. The energy I had to put into all this left me even more drained and less able to meet Jemma's needs. It certainly did nothing to help my relationship with her, although I don't think that was seen as a key objective by anyone. They just needed us to keep her safe and to carry on coping.

All that is in the past and the key question now becomes: how could these relational problems have been avoided and how could it be better for other families in the future? I hear on an almost weekly basis about other adoptive parents in similar conflicts with services, and so I know the problem persists.

I consider myself fortunate to have had counselling training and to have good, regular counselling supervision in which I can explore the way I relate to clients, offload and look at my own issues in a safe and non-judgmental setting. Many practitioners do not get this.

I now recognise how the emotional, frustrated and authentic way I related to these professionals probably triggered certain responses in some of them and some might even say this was misguided and unfair. I do, however, find myself in a paradoxical situation. I know that I could have eased some of these relationships had I behaved differently but I fundamentally believe that, as a distressed parent, I shouldn't have to be making allowances for the emotions of the practitioners I turn to for help. If I was back in that same vulnerable situation again, I would probably do the same.

This is something I have been working on in my personal development, but with little change in the way I feel and think. I am still involved with services as I try to advocate for Jemma, and this continues to provide a mixed bag of relational experience. I encounter the same problems but with different twists and turns and, because I am in a far better place emotionally, I am better able to ignore and defend against their potentially detrimental effects. I am left trying to make the most of those relationships that are meaningful and supportive, and accepting and managing those that are difficult. I do this one-to-one, as professionals leave our lives and new ones enter, which is a very common occurrence.

So, while it may not be beyond the wit of humans to find a solution to the problems of hostility between service providers and clients, I think it is probably beyond the emotional maturity of many of us who work as professional helpers, and it will certainly remain a feature of adopter–professional relationships for a long time to come.

Before I move on from this aspect of adopter–child–professional relationships, and although the focus of this book is on my experiences as an adoptive parent, I would like to make one brief comment on Jemma's relationship with service providers as she grew up.

When she crossed the line, numerically at least, from childhood into adulthood, the services responsible for her care also underwent a notable transformation in their attitude towards her. Like numerous young people in need of care services, Jemma's drift into adulthood was gradual and delayed, in contrast to the sudden, massive change in what was available to her.

Over the years I have witnessed several initiatives intended to address the gap in services for young people as they make the difficult transition between child and adult. Most of them just peter out into nothing. What I often observe in mental health is that older teenagers suddenly drop off a cliff and re-emerge some time, even years, later, climbing their way into adult services – services that mostly do not know how to relate to them and seem to place the responsibility on the young person to simply adjust and become an adult.

This change in attitude is triggered by a date of birth and generally has no relationship to the young person's ability, maturity or vulnerability. At a single point in time, the way that the local authority and health service fulfilled their responsibilities to Jemma changed unrecognisably. She lost most of her status as vulnerable and in need of protection and, despite her clear inability to make adult decisions, was expected to do so. When she couldn't do this, it was, obviously, her fault, and she had to face the consequences. Her dependence on us for support and advocacy was also tossed aside and we were told we were not entitled to involvement in her life or to any information. The effects of this manifested in a number of subsequent actions.

Jemma's social worker at the time, with whom she had a really good relationship, contested some of the proposed changes to her care, but her manager quickly replaced her with a new, more compliant worker. Then Jemma's treating clinician announced that, due to her attachment difficulties and problematic relationship with us, she would be best served by having relationships only with professionals from this point on. We were prevented from seeing her for several weeks, even though this was not what any of us wanted. This was not only insulting to us and made no sense whatsoever; it also made Jemma even more distressed and disturbed. No service provider should have been entitled to make that decision. It was abusive, although, as with the majority of cases of organisational abuse, it was not recognised as such. We had to turn to our solicitor to remedy the situation via Article 8 of the Human Rights Act, the right to a family life. This gives an indication of just how powerful and dangerous services can be, and how easy it is for service users to lose their status as human beings.

Returning to my own relationship with her, Jemma is now an adult and her needs have continued to change, and so has our relationship. Regardless of her problems and our difficult life together, she has passed through the same stages as any child, in that she has grown up, become a teenager, become less dependent on her parents and eventually flown the nest. The way she did this was far from conventional and was delayed in many respects but we have slowly moved towards an adult father–daughter relationship, although I am unsure just how 'adult' it will ever become.

Perhaps one of the most significant differences this has brought is in the way that I feel when in her company and away from it. When she was younger, and particularly in those difficult teenage years when she would only be back for weekends and visits, I would feel extremely anxious when she was away, but this would pass and be replaced by sadness when she was with us. I think my anxiety was partly a parent's worry about her being okay and safe, which was quite a normal response, although given its intensity it was probably also a feature of the trauma bond we shared. The sadness at being with her was probably due to the paradox that I loved her so much but often did not enjoy what she brought with her. Home life was stressful and miserable for much of the time that she was around and, although I desperately wanted her to be with us, it's not surprising that I also experienced this with some sadness. These feelings started to diminish once I began to accept that, regardless of her age, Jemma was at last a grown up and not the little girl I held in my mind's eye. Our relationship began to take on a different intensity. This change was also helped along by the fact that we started seeing each other less and less.

When I am not with her now, my anxiety has been replaced by a sadness that frequently creeps up on me, especially when I think about her and all the things that could have been, and the multiple losses that our dwindling relationship represents.

For me, 'being family' is an intensely relational activity and adoption is primarily a relational experience. It has love and trust at its centre and these have to be reciprocal in order for it to work well: that is, we all need to be able to contribute to this endeavour in some way to meet the needs of the whole, and for the needs of the individuals making up the whole to be satisfied. We all give and we all take, and that's how it works.

In Chapter 1, I referred to our visit to Jemma's foster home and how surreal it was 'deciding if we wanted to spend our lives together' when we had only just met. 'We', at that point, meant the adults around her as, clearly, Jemma took no part in our choice to become a family. I have to accept that she now has the right to decide if that's what she wants and also bears the responsibility for any decision she makes. I know this will not be straightforward as she will never be good at developing, managing and holding on to relationships – her ambivalent and disorganised attachment style will be at work, regardless of what else is going on in her life.

There have been several times when I thought our relationship was over: when Jemma left home at 15, when she made the serious allegations against me, when she or other people decided we were not to have contact with her. These were all endings of one kind or another and brought with them an acute sense of loss and a belief that things had changed beyond repair. Each time we managed to rekindle our connection but, despite our repeated readiness for reparation and reconciliation, they have all left their mark.

When we see her, the hugs that some of the professionals have openly criticised as 'immature and inappropriate' have become less spontaneous, and when we call she sometimes doesn't want to speak; she rarely calls us. If I am honest, the only time she really wants us is when she needs something. While this may sound a familiar tale to many parents, I find it is totally different to my relationship with Michael, which has also changed, but certainly not weakened. Although I retain my place as his dad, we also have an adult-to-adult relationship that is built on trust and mutual respect, as well as love and care for one another. I know our relationship will last a lifetime. I have only recently been aware of just how different my relationship with Jemma has become and of its fragility. The trust between us is limited and we do not fully relate as adults; our relationship is largely based on her dependence on Anne and me and, frankly, I find it draining. I am uncertain where it is headed or if it will endure the next significant test, which will surely come along. It appears that the continual and ongoing challenges to it have had a significant impact.

I see Jemma as being in a small boat, attached to the shore by a rope that we spent years making. Every now and then she drifts off, still within earshot, and we manage to pull her back when she shouts. She might even get out of the boat briefly and stand beside us, but this is becoming less common. As time has gone on, she has drifted further out, and for longer, and the rope is getting quite frayed. Also, my grip on it is growing weaker and I am losing my enthusiasm for this monotonous ritual. One day, perhaps, I will notice that she hasn't called out for a while and when I pull at the rope I will feel no resistance and I will find myself standing there, holding just a frayed, broken end... she will be gone.

References

Buber M (2000/1923). *I and Thou* (R Gregor Smith trans). New York, NY: Scribner Classics.

Carnes PJ (1997). *The Betrayal Bond: breaking free of exploitative relationships.* Florida: Health Communications.

Gibb JR (1961). Defensive communication. *Journal of Communication 11*(3): 141–148.

Karpman M (1968). Fairy tales and script drama analysis. *Transactional Analysis Bulletin 26*(17): 39–43.

Lyth IM (1960). Social systems as a defence against anxiety. *Human Relations 13*: 95–122.

Chapter 7
Dreams, risks and realities

When we became Jemma's parents, the good news rapidly spread from within our close family to our wider network of friends and acquaintances. I was surprised by how many people approached us to offer their congratulations and support, and even more surprised by the number who wanted to share their personal link with adoption with us. From adopter to adoptee, each had their own tale to tell. Our dear friend Gwen, with her husband Jack reluctantly in tow, cornered us in the local supermarket and, in congratulating us on Jemma's arrival, delighted in sharing with us how they had adopted their son in the early 1960s. Their story was very different to ours. They adopted Tony at a time when it was still the done thing for young, unmarried mothers to 'give up' their babies for adoption, often under considerable pressure from their family, the church or professionals. Children's homes were, therefore, full of babies and toddlers, and many of the older children were still, shamefully, being shipped to the other side of the world.

Gwen and Jack had found they could not have children and so, as was the culture of the day, they were pointed in the direction of the local children's home by their GP. They spent some hours in a room full of small infants, and Jack sat with many of them on his lap. It sounds like a kind of try-before-you-buy arrangement. When it was Tony's turn and Gwen took him from Jack, they discovered he had left his mark: his nappy had leaked, leaving a dark, wet patch on Jack's trousers. This, they felt, was a sign that it was meant to be – *he* had chosen *them* – and that's how he became their son. It was destiny.

Well, that's how the story goes. I'm sure it was a bit more complicated than that; at least, I hope it was, but in essence they did what most childless couples of that era did if they wanted to start a family. Being married, heterosexual and childless placed you in a pretty strong position as far as adoption was concerned.

The pendulum has swung a long way in the other direction since then. It slowly became culturally acceptable to be an unmarried mother, and so fewer babies were given up. Although more emphasis was placed on keeping children safely with their birth family, more attention was also directed at protecting those thought to be at risk of harm. By the 1980s, children coming to adoption were older and had usually spent their early years going through a range of traumatic experiences. They had invariably been removed from their family because they had been actively abused or the state had decided the level of care they were receiving was not adequate. This left them displaced, distressed and damaged. The safeguarding of children as an objective of society was encompassed in law by the Children Act 1989:

> An Act to reform the law relating to children; to provide for local authority services for children in need and others; to amend the law with respect to children's homes, community homes, voluntary homes and voluntary organisations; to make provision with respect to fostering, child minding and day care for young children and adoption; and for connected purposes.

Alongside this shift in the demographic profile of children waiting to be adopted came a similar shift in attitudes towards the whole adoption process. Despite a happy outcome for Gwen, Jack and Tony, and for thousands of other families like them, it became no longer acceptable or possible to toddle down to the local children's home and choose a baby. Instead, we moved to what was considered to be a more ethical and child-centred approach in which the role of social care was to find families for children, rather than children for families. This is one of the first messages still given to all prospective adopters.

It has become the responsibility of local authorities and voluntary adoption agencies to recruit and assess applicants for their suitability to provide a permanent home to a child up to the age of at least 18. This does not automatically mean that all those who get through the gruelling and emotionally demanding approval process will be matched and placed with a child. That decision remains the prerogative of the professionals who find the families and, ultimately, the matching panel.

There have been so many changes over the years that it's often hard to keep up with 'what's in' and 'what's out' in the landscape of adoption. These seem to parallel the changing understandings in the sector of what adoption is for, its role and how it meets the corporate needs of society. Ironically, most of the people presiding over these developments are not adopters or adoptees.

If you ask an adoptive parent what matters to *them*, what adoption is all about for them personally, you are likely to get answers that are unrelated to many of the historic changes in adoption practice. This is because, although the way things are done and the objectives of the adoption sector have moved on significantly since Gwen and Jack found Tony, some crucial factors have stayed the same. Like us, Gwen and Jack had felt the need to complete their lives by starting a family, and found they were unable to do so. Being a parent is an essential route to happiness for many of us, one that is often taken for granted, and the loss of that dream can sit heavily and obstinately with those of us who are told we will be childless. When Gwen and Jack approached us in the supermarket that day, they were totally unaware of the process we had just been through; that didn't matter. They came up to us because they understood the hope that adoption embodies and, like most adopters, had been motivated by the same dream. So, despite going through a totally different process, at a totally different time in history, we came together in a common understanding of the intense feelings and human needs that this gift of parenthood can meet. This lies at the core of adoption, is unchanging and creates a vulnerability in those of us trying to complete our families in this way.

Finding that all-important match with the child who will eventually become your daughter or son is an emotionally charged activity whenever and however it's done. Choosing a child, as Gwen and Jack had done, was no longer an option by the time we wanted to adopt, but I remember the days before we heard about Jemma, when we would pore over the pages of the monthly adoption magazine, *Children Who Wait*, hoping to spot and get a connection with one of the smiling faces staring up at us from its pages. I can also remember the uncomfortable feeling that accompanied it. It did not feel right – it was too much like catalogue shopping. Children are not commodities there to meet my need, even if that need is honourable and sincere. I fully understand the shift towards finding families for children. For that matter, I expect Gwen and Jack also felt rather uncomfortable choosing their son, even though this was how it was done all those decades ago. Was that why they looked to him for a sign?

One thing that most adoptive parents will agree on is that they had no idea what it would be like at the outset. All the preparation groups, the masses of reading and the opportunities to meet parents who have already had children placed with them, can never convey the reality of living with an adopted child. As one parent told me, at every stage you think you know what it will be like, but you don't really know until it happens.

Awareness and insight are difficult notions to quantify. Just because I am aware of something does not necessarily mean I have insight. I gain insight from personal experience, where my knowledge combines with my feelings. Hence, I might be aware that drinking too much alcohol will give me a hangover but it's only once I've had that experience that I gain insight and understand what it's really like 'the morning after'.

I recognise a progression in my understanding of adoption as I have lived through the different stages as an adoptive parent.

When we made our application to be approved as adopters, I progressed from having *no awareness* about adoption to having a limited and *abstract awareness* of it from talking to social workers, attending preparation groups and gaining knowledge. I learned about the ABC of adoption, the process, and the problems children might come with, depending on the age at when they are placed. In time, I also had contact with other adopters, heard their stories and caught glimpses of the reality of living with an adopted child. This provided me with a better understanding of adoption and a *vicarious awareness*, through the lives of others. Then Jemma was placed with us and I very rapidly moved to a totally different level of understanding where I experienced the reality for myself. I gained *insight* into what adoption is all about. This has shifted over time as we have lived through many different phases of Jemma's growing up into an adult.

This is an important point because adoption provides such an array of experience that it's hard for a newcomer to make sense of it all. Above all, before I make any decision, I want to know what I am getting into, what it will be like and whether or not I will cope. To get an answer to any of those questions will take experience, but all I have to go on when I make that life-changing decision about adoption is second-hand information. Clearly this needs to be unbiased and honest and to reflect the whole picture and not just parts of it.

Statistics have repeatedly shown that adoption is a risky business and that the dreams with which many people start out often do not come to fruition. Based on the data from the Selwyn report (2014) only about a third of adoptive parents end up with the family experience they had hoped for, one 'very similar to many other families in the community'. When prospective adopters start out, these statistics, if they are even aware of them, do not predominate in their thinking. At this stage, their awareness is based on the information and second-hand experience made available to them during their recruitment and preparation. It is, no doubt, also highly influenced by their hopes and dreams of what adoption holds for them. As noted previously, these feelings and the intense human needs that this gift of parenthood is expected to meet are fundamental to adoption and impart a vulnerability to those of us trying to complete our family in this way. It effectively means that we are very, very willing volunteers.

I sometimes regret the advice and encouragement I gave to would-be adopters many years ago, when we were in the early years of our adoption. In retrospect, I realise how biased and misleading this may have been; but perhaps I shouldn't feel so bad, as it's not just those with no awareness who get sucked in to the adoption dream.

I recently sat talking with a couple who were adopting for the second time. Their first child, Alice, had been a delight, had settled well and now, four years later, they felt ready to try for child number two. They knew the risks, on paper at least, and had seen some friends struggle with their adopted children in a way that made them thankful that Alice had been so straightforward. Even though they acknowledged the uncertainty they faced, they still went on to tell me how they couldn't wait to replicate the experiences of the past four years and how great it was going to be. This was even though they knew that, statistically, a problematic outcome was as likely as another good one. Their understanding of adoption as a really fulfilling experience, supported by their hopes and dreams of being parents again and backed up by all the positivity that surrounds the adoption process, had made them unable to contemplate anything other than another happy ending.

I am not judging them. At the start of this book I stated that I am not sure what would have put me off adoption at the recruitment stage, and that statement still holds. I think that, like most adoptive parents, I was fuelled by optimism and hope and held a very simplistic and unrealistic view of what my life would be like as an adoptive parent. If I was coming fresh to adoption in the current climate, I am sure I would still find myself clinging on to anything that offered a fulfilment of those hopes.

Where does this optimism come from? What is it about? Statistically and rationally it makes no sense and yet it is endemic in adoption, even when placements are being considered that carry massive risk for a family and could have a very negative and detrimental effect on all concerned. It is almost like the cultures of corporate denial operated by some organisations, where there are no such thing as problems or failures, just challenges to inspire workers to greater efforts.

In her book *Smile or Die: how positive thinking fooled America and the world,* Barbara Ehrenreich (2010) explores how positive thinking came to dominate the mental life of Americans. She wrote the book after becoming ill with breast cancer, when she discovered that she was not allowed to be angry and sad about her condition and all it meant for her but was expected to be positive, hopeful and thankful, even, for the learning the experience offered her.

Ehrenreich perceives that positive thinking as an ideology has two components – the positive thoughts themselves (seeing the silver lining) and the practice of positive thinking, grounded in the belief that things get better just because we are looking on the bright side.

She perceptively observes that positive thoughts represent optimism, and optimism is not the same as hope. Optimism is a cognitive skill that can be developed through practice; hope is 'an emotion, a yearning, the experience of which is not entirely within our control'.

I agree that positive thinking and hope are two very different attitudes but they collude very conveniently. The hopes and dreams of would-be adoptive parents are emotionally driven and very different from the optimism of adoption professionals with their messages about 'forever families'. Together they mesh into a warm, fuzzy blur that obviates the 'shadow' side of adoption. This is, of course, much more appealing to adoptive parents, so it's hardly surprising that we get drawn into it.

You can see this in the pages of Prospective Adopters Reports (PARs), where one section will indicate an applicant's clear understanding of the extra needs of adopted children and the realities of the impact of abuse and the difficulties this subsequently presents, and another section will describe how they are looking forward to 'just being mum or dad' to a child and how they want to simply give him or her a good home.

No amount of hope and positivity is going to heal the effects of the highly traumatic experiences most adopted children have lived through or smooth the difficulties this will cause to those living with and parenting them. It is also common for parents to uncover key facts about their children only once they have been living with them for some time, when they become evident in their child's behaviour. These facts have often been known all along by the adoption and safeguarding authorities but either their significance was not understood or they were not disclosed because they were seen as irrelevant or not for general knowledge. In this way, useful and predictive information about a child, even when it exists, is not taken into account during matching or disclosed to the adoptive parents. Hope and positivity once again seem to overrule common sense and ethics.

Jemma was described as needing an adoptive home where she was the only child or the youngest by a margin of some years. This is a common matching requirement, and she did need a lot of time and attention; it was always going to take a lot of energy to parent her. I have often wondered, however, how much better it might have been for Jemma if she had been placed in a much busier household than ours. She was a 90mph child and was placed in our 30mph family, where she had no role models or playmates of a similar age. Our life was calm and sedate, some might even say boring, until she came along, and was totally at odds with her previous life in the care system. It must have been a terrible shock for her, and she never did settle into the peace and tranquillity we tried to create. Also, as she became the focus of all our attention, her outbursts and extreme behaviour had a much greater impact than they might have done if they had been diluted within a larger, noisier family unit, where tantrums and everyday trauma might have been more readily absorbed.

I am not suggesting that any of these suppositions are valid and I can see the arguments against them but, as an adoptive parent, I have found many of the assumptions made about Jemma's needs and our adoption of her were based on relatively weak evidence and accepted operational norms, rather than on careful and informed consideration. In the world of adoption there is too little questioning of the status quo: people do as they have always done. As a parent, I have found this frustrating, never more so than when we looked for therapeutic help.

The problems many adopted children and their families face are extreme and complex and require complex solutions. Over the years, Jemma has been on the receiving end of many 'interventions' and has had therapy with several therapists. With one she made up a life story that she was adopted at 12, had several brothers and was struggling to stop smoking. The fact she has never smoked did not stop her being enrolled on a stop-smoking course – twice. With another, she took on the persona of a girl she once knew. In most of these relationships she apparently told each therapist that this was the first time she felt truly listened to, as was evidenced in their reports. Regrettably, most of these practitioners were simply out of their depth and didn't know it.

In addition to a streak of devilment that may have been at work, basically Jemma just did not trust any of these people. She has, however, a special talent for rapidly working out what any stranger wants of her. She then tells them exactly what she thinks they want to hear. Possibly she hopes that, by doing so, she can stay safe.

In reality, regardless of any anecdotal evidence, an hour or two a week alone with even a competent therapist is going to change very little for children like Jemma, who have serious trauma and separation issues. It could even cause more harm than good, especially if the parents are excluded from the process. Social workers and other professionals seem also to believe that they can take a short course in therapeutic techniques and 'do therapy' with these extremely complex, traumatised children. This misplaced confidence spreads well beyond adoption and is a very disturbing phenomenon in the helping professions.

It took me four years of study and practice to qualify as

a therapist. Even then I was a novice and, although I am now more experienced, I still do not work with children and young people as my qualification is to work with adults. I think most people would be horrified if I took a short course in paediatric nursing and then tried to treat their child's broken leg. So why do some professionals think they can become competent therapists overnight? I can see how this extra training might complement their work and be helpful in some situations, but it is also potentially dangerous if they regard it as a licence to practise beyond their competence. I wonder how many unsuspecting parents believe their child is getting expert help when they are not.

When we were finally offered the right help for Jemma in the form of adoption and attachment-based family therapy with a specialist, adoption-based organisation, she did make progress, and this was the first time we saw a real difference in her. It was remarkable. She stopped her regular attacks on Anne and we began to have proper eye contact with her. She began to process some of her trauma and find new ways to deal with it. The therapy was not for an hour once a week; it included days and days of work with a highly qualified multidisciplinary team, in which we all took part. Drama, artwork, occupational therapy, talking and play therapy all came into their own as the team set about helping Jemma and us with the different aspects of her difficulties. We had really needed this input several years earlier and, although it began to pay dividends, it came too late and then was interrupted several times when Jemma was moved around the country and by the court battle that the local authority pursued in trying to obtain a care order.

In those heady days of pre-adoption optimism, I would never have predicted that Jemma would leave home so abruptly and so chaotically. Disruption, and the feelings associated with it, is, understandably, an aspect of adoption that is particularly close to my heart; whatever changes and improvements are made to the current model, a number of adoptions will inevitably end up in crisis of one kind or another. What happens if, despite everyone's best efforts, an adoption still falls apart? The agency will have had its fee; a statistic may or may not be recorded. But what about me, the adoptive parent?

Adoption breakdown can have devastating effects, in both the short and the long term. If an adoption breaks down very early on it will usually, but not always, be recorded as a disruption. Adoptive parents deserve the utmost compassion when this happens but, in my experience, they are just as likely to be criticised and held to blame. Whether this is justified or not, it is worth remembering that it was never their intention to add another layer of trauma and loss to their own lives or to that of any child placed with them. That was not the plan.

If a disruption is recognised as such by a placing authority, best practice dictates that a disruption meeting takes place, in line with agreed guidelines. Again, this does not always happen as it isn't mandatory. The meeting, if held, should review what happened and why the adoption broke down, in the hope that lessons can be learned and future failures avoided. Unfortunately, the outcome can also restrict or remove the chances of the adopter having another child placed with them. Even if it is retrospectively clear why things went wrong – that risks were underestimated by services, that information about the child was totally incorrect or never passed on – it can still affect the adopter's chances of a further placement. In an equal world, where adopters are valued, this would be done differently and consistently across agencies.

Consistency is something that is often absent from people's experiences of adoption; you never know how the authorities are likely to respond. While I was writing this book, we were contacted by Jemma's latest social worker, a new professional in her life whom we have never met. She emailed us and told us that Jemma wanted to trace her birth mother.

We had always expected Jemma would want to do this at some point, had talked to her about it and of our hope that one day we, all together, could embark on this stage in her life. It came as quite a surprise that some stranger would now be helping her to take this important step. We asked some questions about how the tracing was going to be done and received a quite formal email back. The worker talked about Jemma's rights and pointed out that she couldn't share much about what was going on as it was Jemma's information. This was mildly insulting as we are all too aware of Jemma's rights and have had them quoted at us on many occasions. The social worker also asked for some sensitive third party and personal information from us, which she considered also to be Jemma's and not ours.

When we spoke to Jemma, it became clear that she did want us to be involved but was worried about how we would react. This was bound to be an emotional, challenging and potentially hazardous time for her; we wanted to be there for her in whatever way she needed us. Our main concern was that she stayed safe and was not hurt further. We persisted with Jemma's worker and eventually were included in what became a long, drawn-out process.

I understand that Jemma's worker knew nothing of us or our relationship with her but, to me, to be excluded from this important piece in Jemma's jigsaw felt like a final disenfranchisement as her parent. Although it worked out in the end, my feelings and needs as an adoptive parent were deemed largely irrelevant.

Without doubt, becoming an adopter is a risky business but the good news is that it doesn't have to be. We do have the knowledge and experience to significantly reduce those risks and improve outcomes, especially for families in the third group, where adoption goes disastrously wrong. We can move towards a more informed, intelligent and emotionally mature way of working.

Most people come to adoption because, like our friends Gwen and Jack all those decades ago, they simply want to be a mum or dad and offer a child a loving home. The essence of this has not changed, just as the basic human desires and aspirations that underpin this behaviour have not changed. What does need to change, however, is the way we support biologically unrelated children and parents to do this. We need to make sure that the only economy operating here is a human one and that the main focus is on the parent–child relationship.

This sounds straightforward but is immensely complicated, with intricate emotional dynamics and intensely challenging behaviours on all sides. My hope is that people working in adoption listen to the people living with adoption – all of them, not just the ones that fit the idealised stereotype. Then we might be able to move forward, make better decisions, with better outcomes, and improve the lives of parents and children, forever.

References

Ehrenreich B (2010). *Smile or Die: how positive thinking fooled America and the world*. London: Granta.

Selwyn J, Wijedasa D, Meakings S (2014). *Beyond the Adoption Order: challenges, interventions and adoption disruption*. Bristol: University of Bristol.

UK Parliament. *The Children Act 1989*. [Online.] www.legislation.gov.uk/ukpga/1989/41 (accessed 15 June 2018).

Chapter 8
Adoption and the system

When we adopted Jemma and first began to realise just how difficult this was going to be for all of us, our social worker openly acknowledged that the outcome for any adoption was 'pot luck'. By this she was referring to the many unknowns that exist in adoption, including how a child will develop and be affected by their genes and past experiences, how any specific adopter will be able to cope with the challenges this creates, and the many imperfections in the process of matching adoptive parents with a child. In her view, we had been unlucky.

We adopted many years ago but the fundamental process of finding families for children is pretty much the same today. It is still based on what I, as an adopter, can bring to the table that will meet the needs of a specific child. While information technology has helped with the practicalities of sharing parent and child information, and the growth in our knowledge of the impact of trauma has changed the way things can be managed post-placement, the process itself has changed little.

At the start of this book, I stated what I consider to be the obvious: adoption doesn't just involve a child, it takes an adoptee *and* an adopter. Both parties deserve equal consideration and respect in terms of what this will mean for them; both are entitled to have their individual vulnerabilities acknowledged and steps taken to mitigate possible harm. Unfortunately, this has not been a feature of the current adoption system, which has developed, rightly, to protect and meet the needs of looked-after children.

All children deserve the security of a loving home but the fact that some children cannot cope with the emotional demands of 'normal' family life is rarely taken into account. What might seem like an idyllic new home to us adults, with a new mummy and daddy ready to lavish love and attention, might present as a scary and confusing emotional challenge to a child whose experience of life has been totally contrary to this. For these children, what we think of as a bed of roses can feel like bed of thorns. And reparenting, as it has become known, which helps the child ultimately to experience home life as soft and comforting, does not work for all traumatised children, regardless of the dexterity and intensity with which it is applied. Some children just can't hack it and adoption is not always positive for them, or their new parents.

One of the benefits of adoption that is often mentioned is the breaking of repeating cycles of abuse. Transgenerational trauma within families is well documented. However, rather than breaking these corrosive patterns of parenting, adoption can also create new ones; adopted children can introduce trauma into the lives of their adoptive parents and siblings, which then gets repeated in a new cycle within their adoptive family unit. Disruption and adoption breakdowns are a lot more common than is generally advertised, and permanency through adoption is not always the best way to provide care for every child.

These facts will probably elicit hostility from some, as they clash with the generally held view of adoption as a noble and positive act of rewarding sacrifice. I can understand where this originates but this restricted view has resulted in the whispered screams of many damaged parents not being heard and has left me wondering just why the basic facts seem so scary. As reported in Chapter 4, adoptive parents have a vast range of differing experiences, on a continuum from utter joy to total despair and everything in between. This was more than evident from the 2017 BBC Radio 4 *File on Four* survey. As noted in Chapter 4, while more than a quarter of families reported a very positive, fulfilling and sustainable experience, roughly the same number were in crisis and some two-thirds had experienced violence from their child. These wide-ranging experiences are very well known in the adoption community and ignoring this basic fact does not help families. I think that we need to allow for this in any model of adoption and face up to the immense challenges some children present in terms of behaviour and their ability to take part in family life.

In the foreword to Sophie Ashton's book, *The Secrets of Successful Adoptive Parenting* (2016), adoption expert Bryan Post talks about the internal struggle social workers can experience when faced with the task of disclosing to a prospective adopter the true challenges they are likely to face. He suggests they worry that they will scare off the adopter. This, he argues, is a mistake that can only lead to later problems, some of which could have been avoided.

I have many friends and acquaintances working in the adoption sector and I doubt they would uniformly agree with this view. Most, if not all, would rapidly draw your attention to the hard facts presented to prospective adopters during the assessment process, and none of them went into adoption work with government targets predominant in their mind or with any intention to mislead anyone. They universally feel passionate about children in care and the opportunities that open up to them through adoption; this is why they do the work. I would not want to challenge or change those ideals, but there seems to be a constant bias towards the positive and, for me, the gains and losses don't always seem to be held in balance. I know that some find it hard to fully contemplate or acknowledge that, for a sizeable minority of parents, adoption stinks. It stinks of trauma. Perhaps they have to deny these bad outcomes as a way to contain their own anxiety, because none of them would like to think of any harm coming to the parents or children they are trying to help. And perhaps, like the prospective adopters themselves, they hold a belief that everything will work out fine.

Even if we ignore the third of adoptions that, like ours, do not end well, there is still a very significant flaw in current adoption thinking. It may be true that children need permanency, but thinking of adoption purely in this vein vastly underestimates some of the dynamics involved. Becoming a parent and bringing up a family is not simply a job; just as children are not commodities to be picked over and selected, I am not a commodity, a service, even if I offer myself up as one, and especially if I offer myself up in a vulnerable, undefended and needy state, as do the majority of adopters. It strikes me that the notions of finding children for families and finding families for children are both equally flawed.

I know that most people don't actively think of adoptive parents as commodities. Nonetheless, the process and even the language of adoption, in which I am recruited as 'an adopter' to be matched with a child who needs a home, implies that I have a very specific use that others will decide whether or not to confer on me. I am assessed on the basis of what I have to offer a child until they are 18 years old and on my perceived motivation, but not on *my* needs as a parent and a human being. Despite the much-advertised long-term nature of adoption, what seems to be on most agencies' minds is the here and now. 'Speeding up adoption' has become the goal in recent years: getting children out of care and into adoptive homes as soon as possible. Whether my needs will be met through this, the impact it might have on me and the long-term viability of the family I am able to provide for the child are left pretty much in the lap of the gods. Adoptive parents unwittingly take on a lot of personal risk, and no one in the adoption industry seems to acknowledge this.

I see this from the other side of the fence when I periodically sit on an adoption panel. I often have a pang of guilt when I consider what a difficult placement might do to the caring, hopeful and often evidently naïve applicant in front of us, but this does not feature in our decision-making. There is only one question that seems to matter: based on the evidence before us, do we think they can adequately care for a child into adulthood? I notice how often we panel members reveal our doubts through comments like, 'They should be alright so long as they are matched with a fairly straightforward child,' knowing full well that straightforward children are rare in the adoption world. Any reservations we have are left to be dealt with at the next stage of the process, by the matching panel; the applicants are usually approved (those deemed unsuitable having already been screened out by this stage) and are extremely grateful. We then move swiftly on to the next willing volunteer.

In our defence, I could argue that this is the point; applicants *are* volunteers and we are providing exactly what they want. They are adults, after all, and capable of making their own decisions. However, I suggest that, at this time in their lives, they are also very vulnerable and deserve the same degree of concern and care that we afford to the children we are placing. I am left thinking that, in the pursuit of permanence for children, the system has failed adopters, and we need to change the way that we in the adoption sector think and operate. We need to place a lot more attention on the needs of adoptive parents and long-term outcomes for the whole family, rather than just the (relatively) short-term needs of the child.

I read some briefing papers from CoramBAAF, a leading adoption and fostering organisation, that helped me clarify my feelings on these quite subtle yet profound nuances in the way adoption is viewed.

One of these documents, *Regionalisation of Adoption Agencies: 10 views from the bridge* (Simmonds, 2016a), talks about the reorganisation of adoption services and declares that 'early, evidence-informed care planning and decision making are at the heart of adoption'. Another, *Permanence: a partnership over time between the UK and USA* (Simmonds, 2016b) talks about permanence and the fundamental needs and rights of children, the need for secure and loving families and the importance of placements with carers who have a lifelong perspective – all admirable aims. It also talks about the child's 'psychological parent'. This is a concept developed by law professor Joseph Goldstein and psychoanalysts Anna Freud and Albert Solnit. It is described in their book *Beyond the Best Interests of the Child*, published in 1973, and relates to children identifying who their 'real' parent is, who may not be their biological parent. In a nutshell, they define this as usually the person who cares for the child and whom the child feels closest to; the person who becomes the focus of the child's deepest emotions and whom he or she feels they cannot do without. This is the most important relationship in the child's life, within which he or she can be all of him- or herself and learn, grow and develop. While different people in a child's life can become their psychological parent, life events and prior experiences can strongly influence how any new such parental relationships develop. This thinking runs hand in hand with the ideas expressed in attachment theory by Bowlby and Ainsworth.

These CoramBAAF briefing papers made me quite cross, as do a lot of the things I read about adoption. I do understand the need to consider the child's perspective and give this the highest priority, but papers like these promote ideas and ideals that all too often grate with my real-life experience as a parent. My motivation to adopt did include an element of wanting to do some good, which I think is common to most adopters (we believe we are good people who can offer a needy child a secure and loving home). There is, however, far more to it than that. I did not come to adoption because I wanted to be recruited as a caregiver, a substitute or a therapeutic parent. I was not thinking about what I was doing in terms of placements, permanence or care-planning. I came to adoption because I wanted to be a dad again. Not only that, but I had been told that this is what was on offer. I was lured by the chance to be a 'forever daddy'. I certainly had not considered this would stop when my adopted son or daughter became 18 and, presumably, no longer needed parenting. Probably like the vast majority of adopters, I approached this from a totally different direction to that often taken by professionals.

When I read professional views such as these, I feel invisible. I want to stand on my chair and start waving and shouting, 'Oi… Over here! Can you see me? Do *I* have anything to do with this thing called adoption?' I say again, I am not a commodity or simply a caregiver; that is not what I signed up for. As far as I am concerned, the parent–child relationship is at the heart of adoption, not care-planning.

If it was a desirable outcome for Jemma to bond with me as her psychological parent, does that not imply I have rights in this relationship and that she could also become my psychological daughter? The concept works both ways.

Not everyone comes to adoption for the same reasons, and for those whose motivation does not come from an inability to conceive children by natural means, the permanency model may work. However, there is a fundamental mismatch between the needs of the system and the needs of most adoptive parents. I think this whole area needs some fresh thought and redefinition.

Once approved, prospective adopters and their social workers are free to search adoption databases for a possible match with children who are waiting to be adopted. This can take some time. Some will be fortunate, and a child may have even been identified prior to their final approval, but not all are immediately swept up by placing authorities, eager to secure them as parents. It is still very much a sellers' market. Adopters who have waited to be matched without success sometimes widen the goalposts they have set around the ages, types of children and behaviours they think they can accept. They might also attend activity and fun days arranged by local authorities, at which they will meet many children waiting to be adopted, in the hope that they will make an emotional connection with one or more. The children at these events have, generally, been 'hard to place'.

Most looked-after children have suffered a range of traumatic experiences and these are outlined in Child Permanence Reports, which summarise their profiles and history and are produced by adoption agencies to help adopters decide whether to proceed with the matching process. 'A degree of uncertainty' about a child's future development frequently gets a mention in these reports but the information they provide is often very patchy and can resemble that given by estate agents ('the property is in need of some redecoration', probably indicating that it was last given a lick of paint and new kitchen cabinet doors in the 1960s).

This general lack of clarity perhaps conceals some well-known facts that are worthy of careful consideration, because there is often less uncertainty about these children than is implied. It is well known that trauma often starts *in utero*, via maternal stress, alcohol and drugs; a very large number of children who have experienced extreme neglect and/or violence from birth onwards are going to have very severe and ongoing behavioural problems, and many children who have witnessed or experienced sexual abuse go on to exhibit problems of sexualised behaviour. Many of these children are going to be aggressive to some degree. Such behaviours are far more predictable than these reports would have us believe.

When approved adopters are identified as a possible match with a child, or they themselves identify a child they are interested in, there is a declaration of interest and negotiations begin with a sharing of information. At this stage, it can all get very tense.

Hopefully the adopters' Prospective Adopters Report (PAR), prepared by their social worker, shows that they have stable lives and good relationships, understand on some level the information they have been given and have some experience of looking after children. There is a section on vulnerabilities but in my experience this is often quite superficial and any potential problems are discussed only in terms of how they could affect permanency; the reports concentrate very much on the positives.

The matching panel judges the ability of the adopters to take on the difficult job of caring for an adopted child, based on information in the PAR and by asking questions of the social worker and the applicants when they come before them. Great attention is paid to evidence that the adoptive parents have been taught the basics of child development and can understand some of the feelings of traumatised children, but little attention is paid to whether the applicants will understand and manage their own feelings and responses to the behaviours they may encounter. The applicants have no psychological assessment and scant consideration is given to what adoption could do to them, their relationships or their lives. An assumption seems to be made that adoption will be good for them, that becoming an adopter is like receiving a gift of some kind.

Once a child is placed, a Linking Report is produced. These reports briefly describe the child and the early stages of the placement and are, mostly, glowing portraits of yet another successful outcome: the approved adoptive parents now have a child and another child has been taken out of the care system. These reports are usually prepared within weeks of a placement, when no one knows how the adoption will turn out, how the parents will really cope and whether they will end up in the first, second or third group described by Selwyn and her colleagues in their 2014 study. This is especially disappointing when the factors that make an adoption highly risky and potentially traumatic are very well known. We still let adopters sleepwalk into predictably disastrous placements. If we incorporated what we know today about adoption and traumatised children into a far more intelligent matching process, some of these risks and future heartaches could be avoided.

A small number of agencies are, thankfully, changing their practices on how this is done and, although they generally still maintain the 'families for children' philosophy, they do expend a great deal of effort and expertise in carefully considering the gifts, strengths and vulnerabilities of prospective adopters from an attachment and psychological perspective.

They have incorporated what has been learned from neuroscience and psychology into a much more considered, informed and sophisticated approach to matching children and parents in a way that is safer and more fulfilling for all. They have moved a very long way, for instance, from making the assumption that, simply because an adopter has a good relationship with their own parents and seems to have enjoyed a securely attached childhood, this will magically rub off on any traumatised child placed with them, enable them to re-parent the child and enable the child to form a similarly healthy attachment to them; this may help, but it is not the be-all and end-all of successful parenting. These forward-thinking agencies also spend a lot of time digging through the history of any child they are considering for a match, looking for hidden information and trying to predict how the child might present in terms of challenging behaviour in the future and what it will take to parent them therapeutically. They also recognise the fact that placing a child with the right adoptive parent is only the start of the agency's work so, while many agencies still concentrate the bulk of their efforts on recruiting, training and then placing children with adopters, some are directing more of it into post-adoption support. All these measures reduce some of the uncertainties inherent in the pot-luck model. In the past, only a few agencies who are generally concerned with 'hard to place' children (those most likely to present the greatest challenges to any adoptive parent) have taken this more thorough approach. However, more recently there has been a general shift in this direction with the introduction of the Adoption Support Fund (ASF), which, as the name suggests, has made money available to develop and provide this much needed long-term aftercare.

While these pockets of change are welcome, there is still a very long way to go before a sophisticated model of matching that draws on all the recent advances in understanding about in vitro and early childhood trauma becomes common practice among adoption agencies.

The ASF is both a good example of an improvement and an indication of the massive need that exists within the current system. It also shows how even new developments can be dragged off course.

The Department for Education (DfE) oversees the fund, which can be accessed after placement and is primarily intended to fund therapy and support for adopted children and training that will help their families understand their needs and successfully re-parent them. However, direct help for the adoptive parents is not covered under its terms. Its purpose is to help maintain adoptees with their adopters; it is child-centred, not necessarily family-centred. The DfE increased the fund's budget to £23 million in 2016 in response to an 'unprecedented' demand that saw the fund being consumed at a rate of £500,000 per week. It introduced what it called a 'fair access limit' of £5,000 per child. Most adopters would not be quite as surprised as the DfE seemed to be by the take-up rate. Under current adoption legislation, local authorities have a duty to provide an assessment of the post-adoption support needs for each child they place but have no duty to provide anything by way of help once those needs have been identified (Fursland, 2016). Provision of services to individual families 'is at the local authority's discretion' (Lane, 2006). Although this can be challenged, many still do not provide this much-needed help, as many adopters will tell you. The provision of effective post-adoption support is therefore inadequate and patchy – a postcode lottery. This is what makes it vital that the ASF continues to be funded and managed so it best meets as much need as possible for as many as possible.

Although all adopted children are supposed to have a support plan when they are placed with adopters, this is often vague, and the fact that the placing authority has no legal responsibility to supply anything that has been identified in the plan is, to me, farcical. The support plan has no contractual currency; it is literally just a piece of paper. As a new parent already facing a lot of uncertainty, I would want my child's needs not just to be identified but to be met by the placing authority.

Predictably, I have heard mixed responses from parents and practitioners who have got funding from the ASF. The majority of parents who used it in its first year found that the support it allowed them to get was indispensable. This was mostly specialist therapeutic input for their child. However, since the introduction of the access limit and the requirement for matched funding from the local authority, some parents have encountered problems. Regardless of what was identified at placement, an 'assessment of need for adoption support services' has to establish that help is required, and sometimes social workers seem not to appreciate the level of difficulty families are in. Then, there are several further stages to go through before support is agreed and money is released. This takes time, and the responses from local authorities and the management company that controls the fund can be unpredictable. Some parents report that much of their budget has been eaten up in assessment fees of one kind or another, leaving little for actual therapeutic interventions. The initial euphoria about the fund has slowly turned to cynicism.

Specialist help of the kind that was eventually provided for Jemma comes at a price. The ASF access limit of £5,000 is low, given the level of intervention some of these children will need, and will probably only be of help to those experiencing low to moderate levels of difficulty. It would take more than 10 times that amount to provide a year's therapy and support for a very disturbed child. This would arguably be money well spent but that is difficult to prove as there are no published statistics on the financial cost of failed adoptions, whether to the public purse or to parents. In our case, for instance, although we bore the financial brunt of parenting Jemma for almost 13 years, when things finally fell apart, the costs associated with what came next simply rocketed. In one year alone, we know that more than £200,000 was spent on her care and this did not include the hidden costs of the professionals involved in the court battle the local authority embarked on. I would expect the total cost of Jemma's care to pass beyond the £1 million mark while she is still in her 20s. And we are not an unusual or isolated case. I do not believe that the financial consequences for the taxpayer of failed adoptions like ours feature in the government's accounting practices, or that anyone has even bothered to calculate the true cost of those outcomes.

This leads me to think about the wider context of how the current adoption model is financed and the impact this could be having on parents and children. It would be naïve to ignore the fact that, despite being part of the public sector, adoption services now operate, as does all public service provision, like a business. The adoption industry has to achieve business objectives as well as human ones, and with an inevitable impact.

At the highest level, we all fund adoption through our taxes. That money is distributed by central government through various channels down to regional and local areas, feeding both local government and third sector voluntary adoption agencies (VAAs). Funding is usually secured by tender. VAAs are a part of the system that the government is keen to promote as intrinsic to its regionalisation agenda. They get nothing for recruiting and assessing potential adopters; they only get paid if a child is placed with adopters whom they have approved. The recommended amount for this inter-agency fee was set by the Consortium of Voluntary Adoption Agencies in 2011 at £27,000 for one child, £43,000 for two and so on, to be paid in stages up until the adoption order is made, when the adoptive parents take over financial responsibility for their child and remove the burden from the state. Hence, it is assumed that taking children out of the care system brings long-term benefits to the public purse. The impact assessment of the Children and Social Work Bill, published in May 2016 (DfE, 2016), suggested these would amount to 'possible savings of £310 million across the whole sector' over 10 years, as a result of the regionalisation of adoption services, and including reduced costs from economies of scale and the creation of a larger pool of potential adopters, reducing the number of children and length of time they spent in foster care.

This clearly puts strong pressure on agencies to place children with adopters, in order to get paid. Meanwhile, a zero value is placed on the work they do in the assessment and preparation of adopters. Why are agencies not paid for this activity too? They put considerable time and effort into recruiting, assessing and, most importantly, ensuring that applicants are as well prepared as possible for the realities of adoption. Not all applicants will be suitable and not all, for a range of reasons, will end up with children, but VAAs receive no reward for this important work that should ensure the most unsuitable adopters are identified early on. In this model, adopters are simply a means to achieve the government's ends, rather than a central part of adoption – commodities, in short.

I am not suggesting that money is the only driver for all those running and working in adoption organisations but it is important to at least recognise the financial incentive, and the fact that there are jobs to be had and careers to be made within this industry. The organisations' survival depends on securing contracts at the lowest cost, meeting targets, and finding enough adoptive families with which to place children. How can that be right?

Legally, the system supports this attitude. The Adoption Support Regulations make clear that now my child is an adult, and even before that, once our adoption broke down, I was not entitled to any adoption-based support. My daughter and her birth parents, on the other hand, continue to have access, in theory at least, to a range of adoption-led services.

Thankfully I did have support at various stages in the past, due to the care and diligence of some of the professionals involved, but technically this was not mandated. Now I find myself as the adoptive parent of a seriously troubled adult adoptee, in a position where I continue to care for her at a distance and where I am also traumatised by this whole experience, but where I am not entitled to any specialist help. This enforces the message that I am, indeed, a commodity, but now a redundant one. I no longer serve a useful purpose.

Adoptive parents are entitled to the same rights as anyone else to care and support; it is not just the child and their birth parents who are permanently affected by adoption; adopters are equally affected and some will need help on an ongoing basis because of it. Many find themselves emotionally scarred, traumatised, physically unwell or financially crippled following a very difficult adoption. There is little direct provision for their needs while the child is with them, and none after.

I do realise that, in whatever choices I personally make as an aspiring parent, I can't expect to be protected from myself, but we, as a society, have choices about how we approach adoption. We can choose how we protect families from the potential consequences of being overly hopeful and vulnerable; we can write off the poor outcomes as unavoidable collateral damage, or we can set about trying to do something different. It seems to me that the latter is the only ethical way forward. To do this, we will have to painstakingly unpick and challenge the positive bias in the current way of doing things, admit to the disappointments and disasters, and come clean about what failed adoption experiences truly represent.

Two decades have passed since Jemma came to live with us and, in that time, little has really changed in the wider adoption policy and practice world. Yes, the process of recruiting and processing adopters has speeded up and a lot more information about the impact of trauma is known and passed onto adopters but, had we been adopting Jemma today, I fear we would have ended up pretty much in the same boat: initially drifting along in the euphoria of achieving our hopes and dreams but soon heading into storm clouds that would rock our whole existence. And despite what is now known about childhood trauma and fed to adopters during their preparation, once that storm hit, we would probably still find ourselves feeling quite alone, surrounded by professionals, many of whom could not understand how dire the straits were that we were in and who were ill prepared to help us. 'What did you think you were doing, going sailing in the first place? Didn't you know the risks?' Well, frankly, no.

I see myself as part of the hidden collateral damage created by the way the adoption system currently works. I am part of the shadow side of adoption that dares not speak its name, for fear of being accused of negativity or frightening the horses. And so, like the thousands of other adopters who also sailed this route, or ones very much like it, I sit alone, wondering if I am the only one.

References

Ashton S (2016). *Secrets of Successful Adoptive Parenting.* London: Jessica Kingsley (foreword by Bryan Post).

Department for Education (2016). *Children and Social Work Bill: impact assessments*. [Online.] London: Department for Education. www.parliament.uk/documents/impact-assessments/IA16-008.pdf (accessed 26 April 2018).

File on Four (2017). *Adoption: families in crisis.* BBC Radio 4. www.listenersguide.org.uk/bbc/episode/?p=b006th08&e=b095rs05 (accessed 26 April 2018).

Fursland E (2016). *The Adopter's Handbook on Therapy: getting the best for your child*. London: CoramBAAF.

Goldstein J, Freud A, Solnit AJ (1973). *Beyond the Best Interests of the Child*. New York, NY: Free Press.

Lane M (2006). *Adoption Law for Adopters in England and Wales*. Banbury: Adoption UK.

Simmonds J (2016a). *Regionalisation of adoption agencies: ten views from the bridge*. CoramBAAF briefing. London: CoramBAAF.

Simmonds J (2016b) *Permanence: a partnership over time between the UK and USA*. CoramBAAF briefing. London: CoramBAAF.

Chapter 9
Life after adoption

It is perhaps perverse to be writing this chapter towards the end of this book because really it was where I started, reflecting on who I am and where I am, now that I seem to be on the far side of adoption. Where do I go from here? Sitting alone, on this foreign, unrecognisable shore, I have had plenty of time to process what has happened over the past 20 years.

My deliberation really started with yet another question: 'How am I?' The answer I came up with was 'Not very well', and being able to acknowledge this fact and reflect on it was the beginning of some positive change for me.

In retrospect, I am not sure I was ever cut out to be an adopter, in the government's and social work sense of the word. I just wanted to be a dad again and thought I could do some good. I also love a challenge... or I used to. I certainly didn't consider I was applying for a job as a carer or as a substitute family.

I am pretty sure, on the other hand, that I *was* cut out to be a parent, and that's what I became through adoption. To restate my point, I became Jemma's parent, not her adopter/carer; for all the reasons I have already explained, I am, and always will be, Jemma's dad, even if this is not in the way I initially envisaged.

You might find those two paradoxical statements confusing. In fact, it may only make sense to parents who have struggled and been injured by their adoption experience.

These days, it seems, everyone is on a journey of some kind or another. I get really tired of hearing this clichéd term, especially when it is applied to adoption, as it so often is. It used to be that we went on a journey to the coast or to see Auntie Mary but now every experience and life event seems to get expressed in this way: we go on a journey of recovery, of discovery, of heartache, or whatever.

For me, adoption is definitely not a journey because that implies there is a destination to be reached. There is no end to parenthood or to the feelings that accompany it; parenthood is not finite. For me, adoption is about experience, process and becoming, not about travelling to an endpoint. In this enterprise I became, and forever will be, Jemma's dad, but what that means to both of us will continue to evolve.

It has not been an easy experience and it has changed me. I hope that now Jemma is an adult I can at least find a calm place where I can continue to become the me of the future. I would hate to be stuck forever holding the emotional turmoil that I've held for the past decade or more. This has largely been self-perpetuating as I am not one for giving up, probably because on some level it represents failure to me and the fact that, by deduction, I am not good enough. Only after all avenues have been exhausted, and I am also exhausted, will I ever hold up my hand and give in.

And yes, alright, I give in. I can't fix Jemma, change her personality, resolve her trauma, save her. I can't stop her behaving destructively. I can't instil in her the capacity for cause-and-effect thinking and I definitely can't change the way she does relationships.

She will survive. Damaged people often survive at the expense of those around them, even if it's in a way that causes them yet more pain and seems illogical. And if I insist on treating her like a vulnerable, fledgling cuckoo, even though she has grown and flown away, then surely, one day, I will be crushed by the weight of it all. I often wonder if the only way to survive is to sever all ties with Jemma and face the pain that this also will bring, but this is easier said than done. Anne and I are the only real source of compassion and constancy in her life and the only ones who care deeply about her, and my core beliefs about what a parent is and does are hard to let go. They eat away at whatever boundaries I put in place and drag me back towards a drama triangle in which I take the role of rescuer and can become a victim at any point. To keep Jemma in my life while at the same time casting off those destructive emotional bonds that entangle us will take fortitude and a level of personal skill that I am still trying to develop. I also need to learn to look after myself.

Self-care is one of the things that adoptive parents are lectured on as a way to preserve their sanity and the adoption. Those promoting this are not usually facing the reality of living with a traumatised child who demands and secures every part of your attention for every minute of the day; a child who is going to fight and challenge you from the second they get up until the moment they go to bed, *if* they go to bed. In the midst of this chaos, it's just about impossible to practise self-care. Now, with Jemma gone, you would think it would be more achievable, yet I confess that this is one skill that I still struggle to perfect.

There is a sense in which I have forgotten how to look after myself. This is not healthy, and it's probably time I resurrected some of the things that I used to enjoy doing or found some new activities to make me happy. After all, I can't change the past and can only go forward, but I don't seem to be getting very far. I feel very strongly that, before I can make any headway, I need to sit and contemplate all that has happened and how it has affected me and come to terms with my feelings about it all.

If I had to find one word to sum up my adoption experience, it would probably be loss. There have also been some significant gains but the things that have affected me most and influenced the way I now feel and think about life all seem to have a loss of one kind or another at their centre.

When Anne and I got married, we talked about having at least three kids, and I had a vision of getting old and having numerous grandchildren who would knock on the door on their way home from school to say hello and raid the biscuit tin. Weeks would be punctuated with babysitting and helping out, and weekends busy with visitors of all ages. I know that this is not how it is for lots of families and is probably more reminiscent of my parents' generation than mine, but I have always had a deep yearning for a large, tight-knit family. Having to let go of that dream is a very considerable loss and it is not the only one; there are many other losses relating to our adoption that are not quite so obvious.

It may sound odd, but I lost my middle age. In the years that most people of my generation were finding more time for themselves and doing nice things, having brought up a young family and probably paid off their mortgage, I was being subjected to daily abuse and spending all my time and energy looking after Jemma and trying to resolve our family's problems.

After 12 years, we still had a toddler in our midst – a very big and aggressive one. Holidays and special occasions were a nightmare that we contained as best we could. My career and finances both suffered. It was like getting up every day and running a marathon through hostile territory. There was no choice about it and no time to nurse yesterday's blisters – I just had to get up and run. This went on for years and left me traumatised, worn out and depressed. Many of my friendships drifted away and I became isolated. Even though the constant running has finally stopped, I now struggle to make new friends. My character has changed and I often feel out of sync with the world and struggle to see real happiness and promise in even the good things in life. It's hard not to notice the parallels between me and Jemma; that stink of trauma still lingers, even though she has left the building.

Another loss is that of not seeing Jemma grow and blossom as a result of our nurturing, and there were many other milestones in raising a child that we never achieved. There were very few birthday party invitations, no sleepovers with friends, no clean transition to secondary school, no GCSEs to worry about or results to collect, no school prom, no agonising over a job or career path.

These losses of what never was were imperceptible to the vast majority of people, but really important to Anne and me. We missed out on so many of the things we had hoped to experience through this gift of parenthood.

I suppose it was like having a child with a disability that no one else can see because Jemma is, to all intents and purposes, emotionally and psychologically disabled. Even we didn't spot this at first, and it took us several years to understand the full consequences of her abusive past. And, just as with any serious disability, our whole family has been affected by it.

The invisibility of Jemma's underlying problems and the general lack of public understanding around adoption was highlighted to me when I was chatting to a woman – I'll call her Jessica – I met at a friend's house. Jessica told me that she was a social worker and, not surprisingly, the fact that we had adopted soon came up. Jessica was unaware of our story and expressed her view that adopted children are the same as all other children and the problems adopters often moan about are down to 'normal teenage behaviour' that they just need to get on and deal with. Anne was there too. The conversation went rapidly downhill thereafter, as you may imagine.

I am constantly disappointed by the confidence with which some people judge others. It's so easy to offer the solution to a problem when you are not the one who's living with it. To acknowledge that your perception of life is based only on what you have personally experienced takes a lot of self-awareness.

Using the theories of Carl Rogers, it might be said that life *is* perception and just because I have experienced life in one form does not mean that all other human beings have done the same or that my way was the right way. My reality is not their reality, and my truth is not their truth, and vice versa.

I try to stay mindful of this in my work and if I listen hard enough, I always learn something new about the world from each person I work with as I get a glimpse of *their* reality. Often, I end up thankful that my version of life has been very different to theirs.

One of my clients, Duncan, arrived late to his counselling one day. He was an articulate, thoughtful, middle-aged man and he apologised for what he saw as 'messing me about'.

Duncan was living in a rundown block of flats known as Barrowfields, having lost his job and family home due to severe anxiety and depression. This type of social decline is common in people with enduring mental health issues. He struggled to get by and had spent most of the previous night listening first to loud music coming from the drug dealer's flat above him and then to a very loud argument in the adjoining property. Barrowfields is not the sort of place where you knock on a neighbour's door to complain in the middle of the night, so he just put up with it and waited for it to stop. He told me that at 3am he was standing on his balcony in his dressing gown, smoking a roll-up and wondering 'whether there is a place on earth that contains all the lost left socks and teaspoons'. His humour concealed his frustration and low mood and, as he later revealed, the fact that he had stood for some time wondering if there was any point to his life at all. It was a long way down from his balcony to the ground.

In those shared moments in the counselling room, I think I came close to understanding what Duncan was feeling and the desperation he faced each day. It also provided a glimpse of how life is for the residents of Barrowfields, but I can still only imagine what it might be like for him to live his life in this way, because for me to gain a full insight into Duncan's world, we would need to trade places. There is simply no replacement for experience.

Comments like the ones Jessica made that day really hurt. They invalidate my life and my experience as an adoptive parent, and present an idealised picture of adoption, possibly because it's too difficult for the speaker to accept the awful truth that for lots of parents this is not the case. Jessica implied that if it all went wrong, it was clearly my fault. I imagine she had never been attacked by her child wielding a knife, or strangled, or pushed down the stairs. How else could she really 'get it'?

Jessica is not alone in her thoughts and lack of insight but being surrounded by people who have no understanding of my experience, projecting a view of life that is totally contrary to the one I know, is very alienating. It adds to my feelings of being out of sync with other people. Perhaps this is partly why I seem to have lost the ability to make and keep new friends.

This loss has an added downside because synchronicity with others is a vital component of my sense of safety. To experience social support, to be truly seen and heard by those around me, understood and cherished, and to reciprocate this in relationship with another human being, plays an important part in my mental health. This is very different to simply being with other people; in fact, without the unconditional acceptance and empathy of others, I would find it hard to remain fully functional.

While Rogers promoted the benefits of these constructive relationships, Robert Carkhuff noted the negative impact of their absence in times of crisis (Carkhuff, 1987; Brazier, 1996). They are vital to my wellbeing and I have noticed the effect that being misheard and misunderstood, judged even, continues to have on me. My adoption experience can sound so bizarre and incomprehensible to most people that I often struggle to perceive any reciprocal and supportive understanding from them. Although I still get on with most people, more often than not, as soon as any new acquaintance hears about my life in any detail, they either glaze over or run a mile. I think that's because they find it hard to process and accept my experience of being a parent, and it frightens them on some level. I also get annoyed by their blissful ignorance of the real world – or, more precisely, of *my* real world. I suppose on some level *I* am also judging *them* and I'm even jealous of the fact that, from where I am standing, their life looks positive, pink and fluffy, a place where good things generally happen and life's challenges have not derailed them and changed who they are.

I am therefore left with the dilemma of either presenting a facade that hides the full extent of my experience or of simply being myself and scaring them off. Neither seems to work very well and I sometimes feel that I am in a tribe of one – perhaps another piece of parallel process.

Of all the losses I could list, the most notable will be well known to parents who have suffered a disruption and seen their child leave home prematurely, often following some horrible and chaotic events. Although in our case this did not mean that we lost contact with Jemma completely, it was still an ending, a bereavement, a loss, and one that has certain unique features. Like someone dying of a slow, debilitating illness, she did not go suddenly; it happened in stages and even now she has not fully gone, but she isn't with us either. This brings with it a level of complexity that, when added to the trauma bond between us, makes it hard to pin down the exact nature of the loss I am experiencing. It also brings the risk that I will develop a form of complex grief that may be difficult to process and escape from.

For me, Jemma's departure started the day I signed the Section 20 papers, once more giving the local authority some rights over her welfare. They could not legally provide the level of respite we needed without this being signed and, although it did not confer any parental responsibility on the authority, thereafter officials often acted as if it did, making unilateral decisions about Jemma's care and not always providing us with important information. In some respects, they treated the Section 20 like a care order and behaved as if we did not exist.

I vividly remember the day I signed this document – the bright yellow room and the blue chairs. Anne could not face the prospect and was unwell, so I had gone alone. It was all very business-like. The papers were prepared and, after a brief meeting with social workers, most of whom I had never met before, they were presented to me to sign. I don't believe the others present noticed the delay as my pen hovered over the last page. They probably thought I was working out where to sign it, but in fact I wondering *whether* to sign it. I don't remember saying anything to them again after that.

They took the completed papers, said goodbye, I think, and left the room. After a few seconds, one of the admin staff came in and escorted me from the building. It was a bright, sunny day and I stood in the car park staring into space for a while until someone passing by asked if I was okay. This jolted me out of my vacant gaze and I got in the car and drove home.

Since then, there have been many further stages in this non-ending: the day Jemma finally left home for good, the period when she made the serious allegations, the times we have been denied contact with her by professionals. With every new stage comes the question of whether this will be the final one but, like some cruel mathematics conundrum, however many times the bond between us is cut in half, it never runs out; we never reach the end.

Living with a loss that is never complete has left me *incomplete*. How can I go about becoming whole again and moving on when so much remains unresolved and uncertain? I can identify the losses but I don't really feel them because they are not, strictly, endings. This pulls me back to an old place that I know well and where I always seem to get stuck.

Many models of how people deal with loss have been proposed by different theorists over the years and, as most will admit, none are definitive because each person and each loss is unique. The model suggested by psychologist William Worden (1983) makes a distinction between grief (the feeling or personal experience of the loss) and mourning (the process that occurs afterwards). He notes that mourning is an active process and one over which we therefore have some level of control, and he provides four tasks that need to be accomplished before we can move on with life. These tasks are fluid except that the first needs to be completed before any of the others can begin. This primary task is one of accepting the reality of the loss. Only then can issues around the pain, adjustment and change brought on by the loss be processed.

Loss and change are often inseparable: you don't usually get one without the other. I know that every change in life has losses attached to it and every loss brings about change, but perhaps I have been looking at things from the wrong end. I have been trying to make changes to my life and be different but that may be impossible until I can resolve and accept some sort of ending with Jemma. So, what's stopping me?

I wonder if, just as Jemma has always held on to her dream of an idealised birth mother, I have continued to hold on to my yearning for an idealised daughter and family? I can see this in my repeated attempts to keep our family together. Had she gone and never returned it might have been different but because she is still in my life, albeit at a distance, I can choose to hold on to the tattered dream of my fairy-tale family. If, on the other hand, I can learn to accept that the dream is really gone and that all I am left with is purely illusion, I may be able to complete the stages of processing its loss.

Working against this outcome is my over-developed sense of parental guilt and the unpredictable way that Jemma keeps coming back into my life, often needing to be rescued. However, I am slowly coming to the sad conclusion that whatever is left of our father-daughter relationship will now have to occupy less space in my life. I know I also have to accept that our relationship will never match my ideals, beliefs and values about parenthood and family. If I can come to terms with these realities, it will probably be as near an acceptance of an ending as is possible.

Even then, to adjust to this new way of seeing things will be a challenge. I will need to take a long hard look at my values and beliefs and who I think I am. I will also have to acknowledge some of my weaknesses and some of the notable changes that have resulted from my experiences over the last 10 years and more.

My reluctance to give in to the inevitable, even when it is staring me in the face, is not the only one of my characteristics that I will need to change. I also have a tendency to worry about relatively insignificant things in a way that is often disproportionate and unhelpful. In truth, I have always been a worrier, just as my mother was before me and her mother before that. It was, incidentally, my mum who helped cause the national sugar shortage of 1974 through her worrying, so I know it has some considerable clout.

Sugar in the 1970s was not the demon foodstuff it is today and, along with millions of other housewives, she was used to piling it into just about every hot drink and dish she prepared. She was horrified by the announcement that supply could *possibly* be rationed and began buying and hoarding pounds of the stuff so that we did not run out. Ultimately, sugar did become scarce, due to massive overbuying – a kind of self-inflicted shortage – and mum then spent weeks giving it away to neighbours who were not of such an anxious disposition and who had not, therefore, stocked up on the white gold. I couldn't quite see her logic.

I can, however, recognise the anxiety associated with the prospect of doing nothing in the face of what my mother perceived as a threat to her family life, however minor. The sugar issue was trivial and mum had many more serious events than this to deal with as I grew up, but that inherently unsettled feeling that she often exhibited is one that I recognise in myself. I too find it really difficult, in the face of a possible and unwanted outcome, not to react. Ironically, and for totally different reasons, her life story was also one of loss; I think it is no accident that we both like to have ordered lives and 'all our ducks in a row', and if one is out of place we feel compelled to do something about it.

This tendency has fuelled the many battles I have waged over the years to try to fix things and get the help that Jemma and our family needed. Unfortunately, in the process of doing this, I have been worn into the shape of a battler, a relentless fighter. I am now so used to conflict that I expect it to happen and have become stuck in that role, even though it no longer fits and I no longer want to occupy it. Unless I change this attitude and learn to take a back seat in Jemma's life, I run the risk of it making me permanently ill.

It's going to be hard to change. My red buttons are still pressed every time I see Jemma put at risk or in distress. Stopping myself from overreacting, getting wound up and jumping out of my seat to charge at the injustice of it all is an ongoing struggle. I am trying, however, to move towards a point of feeling more comfortable with being the father of an adult child whose problems I can't always fix. Those bloody ducks are never going to be in a perfect line.

Another important reason to change the nature of my relationship with Jemma, and with service providers, is that

I keep being re-traumatised. I know Jemma and her support workers don't understand this but it repeatedly erodes my quality of life and makes me vulnerable, anxious and generally unhappy.

Last week, for instance, we had a phone call from Jemma's key worker. We hear very little from her and if we do it is usually because she needs us to provide something for Jemma or needs some information to complete a form or report. The other reason she contacts us is to accuse us of something. Last week's contact fell into that category. Allegedly, we had taken money from Jemma's bank account and this had to be investigated as potential financial abuse. The worker was a little taken aback when Anne acknowledged that, yes, we had moved money from Jemma's account. This was because she has lived in various places since leaving home but kept our address for her benefits and we had periodically helped her move money between accounts at her request. We saw this arrangement as protective, as she had lost a bank card and her PIN and had money stolen while in care; moving her money had limited the damage.

I am unsure what part Jemma took in this latest accusation or if it was purely down to poor communication. We had to spend some hours in email conversation with her key worker, explaining ourselves and pointing out that the financial arrangement had been agreed with Jemma and her two previous workers. The key worker suggested some changes to the arrangement, we agreed to these, and it all blew over.

Such incidents occur with monotonous regularity. It can feel like a form of corporate bullying and there seems to be little end to it. Every time Jemma gets a new worker, it's a lottery whether they will want to engage with us and what attitude they will take.

As discussed in Chapter 6, I believe I have a reasonably good understanding of these relationships. I know that I can come across as determined, questioning and ungrateful, and how easy it is to upset and prompt a hostile response from some workers. Unfortunately, my understanding of these events does not stop them really damaging me.

I had felt fine for some weeks but it took only minutes for this latest accusing phone call to plunge me back into feelings that are part of my trauma signature – predominantly fear, anxiety and anger. If I am to stay a part of Jemma's life, I need to find a way to protect myself from these harmful encounters. This will not be easy but there are signs that I am slowly pulling this off.

I used to react intensely and immediately to every little trigger; my stomach would turn inside out as I plummeted back into those awful feelings of dread. Recently I have noticed that this is reducing and the anxiety that predominated has been replaced by sadness. I have also noticed that, when once I would ruminate about the latest problems all night, I can now set them on one side a lot faster. If I was talking about a physical test and not an emotional one, I would say that my recovery time has improved.

Other things are improving in me too. Looking back, I can see how, as Jemma grew and the level of difficulty we experienced got worse, my life became centred around her and our survival as a family. Most days, and many of those nights when I couldn't sleep, were taken up with very little else and she was rarely out of my thoughts for long. This became unrelenting, day by day, week by week and year by year. There was simply too much to do and too many worries.

A friend who is a martial arts aficionado tells me he uses a form of meditation called Mokuso to clear his head in preparation for combat. He empties his mind; I filled mine with Jemma and this effectively squeezed out everything else. This was not a healthy way to live.

I hesitate to say this but something has been slowly shifting in me: I think that I have freed my mind a little and this has allowed new possibilities to enter it. I am becoming less focused on Jemma, less consumed by her and more conscious of me. I am once more able to focus on some aspects of *my* life – ones that I have been neglecting for years. I now find it easier to talk about my past adoption experiences in a more balanced and meaningful way. This is probably due to the growing distance between me and Jemma and our mutual trauma.

This fresh awareness does highlight certain deficiencies that have developed in me. I have noticed the problems I create for myself by being fairly reclusive, being disconnected from the world and letting life effectively pass me by. I have also become aware of the danger of letting the bad stuff, past and present, contaminate the good stuff, and letting old perceptions of life stop me pursuing new possibilities. I have been trying to reverse this by pushing myself to try new things, take courses, meet new people and generally re-engage with the world at large. It seems to be working. I was recently in a garden centre, the aroma of hyacinths and other spring blooms filling the air and soothing music playing over the heads of relaxed shoppers. For a few moments I actually felt whole and well and, most importantly, at peace. I haven't felt like this for years but occasionally it now returns, and I know this is an indication that I am finding some of my old self. I also noticed that I have recently experienced something that resembles spirituality, or a sense of it, and again this has been absent for a long time. I think I am slowly recovering.

Yesterday I listened to an item on the radio about post-adoption depression. There was a phone-in session afterwards and several parents took the opportunity to call in to share their stories. All were women and all were very upbeat, describing a sometimes difficult but nonetheless wonderful experience. It was also noticeable that they all had young children who had been placed with them in the last few years.

I had a mixed reaction to this. I sat and pondered how, more than a decade ago, Anne or I could have been one of these callers. Not because either of us experienced post-placement depression as such but because we did enjoy some of the euphoria of parenthood for several years. It's hard to remember that at times. It has not been all bad and I can still consider that the early gains offset some of the later losses.

When we were assessed, a lot of effort was put into making sure that we understood and could accept that any child placed with us might struggle to 'perform' at school or to achieve other conventional marks of success. This was seen by the professionals as important for us to understand and take on board, as we needed to be accepting, supportive and non-judgmental parents who would love our child no matter how gifted they were, or not. As it turned out, this was a red herring in the context of the actual challenges of adoptive parenthood. What confounded us was not Jemma's academic performance; it was simply that Jemma was not equipped to be nurtured and parented and loved, and we were not equipped to cope with that reality or to provide what it would take to help her to change her view of the world and of herself. Unfortunately, she is like a big black hole that can never be filled. We could pour all of ourselves into that hole for the rest of our lives and we would just disappear.

I sometimes think about what we could have done differently and I could talk about the 'ifs and buts' of our adoption forever. If Jemma's problems had been understood and flagged up at the very start, if we had been given the right support in a timely manner, if we had been superhuman in our efforts, things might have been different. Regrettably, none of these things happened and, at the end of the day, love was simply not enough.

Since Jemma left us, she has never settled in one place for long, and she continues to have a great deal of involvement with the statutory support services. Like many young people with similar histories, her mental health is very poor and she has had brief scrapes with the criminal justice system. She is often unhappy and her quality of life is far worse than we would wish for her. It is unlikely that she will ever function independently but, somehow, she manages to survive, just.

The metaphor of the pre-flight talk is often used in adoption circles: in an emergency you must put your own oxygen mask on first, before helping your child, because if you pass out, you both become casualties. I have been foolishly struggling for air for far too long while trying to fit Jemma's oxygen mask and it doesn't help either of us. The best thing I can do for Jemma, and for myself, is to make sure my oxygen mask is firmly on so that I can continue to support her. Basically, I need to stay alive and well and breathing, and this means putting myself first and getting on with my life. To Jemma, this might look like I am abandoning or rejecting her but it is the only way we can go forward; otherwise, ultimately, her problems could suffocate both of us. So now, whenever I hold her in mind, it is not as the little girl with bobbles in her hair but as my adult daughter who has all sorts of emotional problems, most of which she has to deal with herself.

On the Friday after Jemma left home and was taken back into the care system, Anne and I went for a long walk around a local reservoir, ending up at a pub for lunch – in peace. We talked about her on that walk, about life and adoption, and also about how much better we already felt knowing that we were not going back home to another round of abuse and chaos. That evening I sat in front of my computer to write my journal and I wondered what she was doing. My fingers ran loosely over the keys.

I recorded many mixed emotions that day. We had been hanging on by our fingernails for some time and so, although it was devastating to see her go, the feeling of sheer relief initially outweighed everything else. This soon changed and a week later I wrote:

> Some days I would wake and just lie there, quietly listening for sounds from the next room, dreading the moment Jemma exploded into the day. This morning I woke early and listened, longing for the sound of movement. And there was none. And I cried.

Perhaps our adoption represents the ultimate paradox: that I both love my child and often can't stand to be around her, and I believe it is no accident that my ambivalence has strong parallels with Jemma's attachment style. Our separation, if that's what this parting represents, was to turn out to be incomplete, like so many aspects of our adoption, and she has come and gone many times since then. Life and my relationship with her have continued to be turbulent and traumatic, and I have had to adapt to the changing situation. My grief has been replaced by a lingering sadness and my hopes by a new reality. I am learning to be different, moving towards re-finding myself and away from being totally consumed by my role as Jemma's dad.

One thing that would help me to move on is the compassionate understanding by others of how adoption has affected my life. I realise I am placing a high expectation on other people in hoping for this, because my story reveals a side of adoption that is seldom talked about and is at odds with the picture that most people, and the state, prefer to see. Nonetheless, it is true. My hope is that in finding my voice as a parent I will finally begin to feel truly heard and understood. Of course, this will only happen if there are enough open-minded people out there who are prepared to listen.

References

Brazier DD (1996). *The Post-Rogerian Therapy of Robert Carkhuff.* [Online.] Malvern: Amida Trust. www.academia.edu/3663201/The_Post-Rogerian_Therapy_of_Robert_Carkhuff (accessed 27 April 2018).

Carkhuff RR (1987). *The Art of Helping.* Amherst, MA: Human Resource Development Press.

Worden W (1983). *Grief Counselling and Grief Therapy: a handbook for the mental health practitioner.* London: Tavistock.

Chapter 10
A better way to build lifelong families

'Relationships are the golden thread running through children's lives.' This was a key message from the 2013 Care Inquiry and one that I think most people would agree with. The relationships we have in childhood underpin all that we become in later life and the critical need for good-enough parenting in our early years, and the consequences of not receiving it, are well researched and documented.

The Inquiry report, *Making Not Breaking: building relationships for our most vulnerable children* (Care Inquiry, 2013), backed up by the accompanying review of research, *Understanding Permanence for Looked-after Children* (Boddy, 2013), provides evidence-based and straightforward recommendations on how we can best care for some of our most vulnerable children.

The report stresses the importance of recognising the different routes to permanence and of ensuring the quality and robustness of each placement so that, whichever option is chosen, the benefits endure throughout childhood and beyond. Adoption clearly features among these options, even though it is right for only a small number of children. Regardless of its comparatively small role, over the years it has attracted more attention, concern and opinion than many other outcomes for looked-after children, and the legislation and policy surrounding it reflect this.

Successive governments have grappled with the issue of caring for looked-after children for decades, producing numerous initiatives, action plans, reforms and legislation. In recent years, these have generally built upon the underlying principles of the Children Act 1989, but many have been reactive, in response to emerging problems.

One thing that is very apparent is that there are many agendas driving adoption. There is a government agenda, a local authority agenda, an agency agenda and a social work agenda, to name but a few, and all of them have their own objectives, even though they may share one stated purpose. Unfortunately, all these agendas do not neatly fit together and many do not simply focus on the ideals set out above. Added to this, they all feed into the underlying cultural attitudes and beliefs about adoption, and these in turn influence adoption practice.

It is important to understand these different agendas and where they originate, because they strongly influence the way new recommendations, such as those from the Care Inquiry, are translated into practice and can forge a disconnect between the good intentions we start out with and how they are played out on the ground. As a result, any new message can turn into the same set of practices, regardless of the original intent.

An added issue for me, as an adoptive parent, is that, in the process of regulating and improving practices, adoption has been highly systemised and theorised. This has served to dehumanise a very human and relational activity – parenting a child. It has also produced a complex system that is focused on function but has, in some areas, lost sight of purpose. I believe the system has come to believe that *it* is at the centre of adoption, not the families it serves.

Nonetheless, there *has* to be a system of some sort and adoption sits within the framework of service delivery for looked-after children as one of the options for providing them with permanent homes.

The Department for Education consultation document, *Improving Permanence for Looked-After Children*, was also published in 2013 (DfE, 2013a). This sought the views of professionals, public bodies, foster carers and children on a range of proposals to 'strengthen the team around the looked-after child; improve the status, security and stability of long-term foster care; and strengthen the requirements for returning children home from care'.

According to the consultation document:

> Achieving permanence is multifaceted. It requires children to experience not only physical permanence in the form of a family they are a part of and a home they live in but also a sense of emotional permanence, of belonging and the opportunity to build a strong identity... The current framework for permanence includes three elements – emotional, physical and legal permanence.

I don't disagree in principle with this, but adoption has some unique features that set it apart from other forms of permanence and I believe there are major pitfalls if adoption is viewed, thought of and expressed only in terms of achieving permanence for a child.

In most families, the relationship – the love and care – between children and parents is not thought of in terms of permanence and is not one-way. The golden thread of relationship has strands from both sides that bind together and its permanence is very rarely questioned by either. A unique feature of adoption is that the thread is woven between two otherwise *unrelated* human beings and starts at a later stage than in most birth families. Additionally, one of the participants has most likely found previous relationships to be more like barbed wire than golden thread. It may take some time and considerable perseverance before these strands begin to bind together.

It is important to understand that permanence and parenthood are two different concepts and adoption is not just about permanency planning for the child. It is about a whole load of other things that go into making a family and being a part of it. Permanence, as it is defined, is an aim and, ideally, a consequence of adoption; it should not be seen as the starting point. From this perspective, perhaps the most significant improvement to adoption practice would be to take the simple, yet hugely important step away from family-finding and towards *family-making*.

This is about more than a simple change in wording. In the pursuit of 'finding families for children', something vital has gone missing from adoption. It has led to the current situation where adopters are 'recruited' as a resource to meet the care needs of the child, and the crucial factor in the success or failure of adoption – the relationship between child and parent – being either assumed or ignored. The sole priority has been to get children out of the care system and into permanent homes; the long-term problems this can create for both parents and children have been deliberately slipped under the carpet. Parents are not commodities and adoption is about forming new families, not finding them. It is not primarily about care provision, providing a safe environment, re-parenting or permanency, even though those are essential elements of the package; it is about the child–parent relationship, and getting this right for both sides is in the best interests of the children.

I realise this does not fit with the adoption industry's view of the world and how adoption is currently done. Any professional reading this will immediately say that the child's needs are paramount and adoption is about the child, not the adopter. I am not suggesting that we lose sight of the child's needs or that they are diminished in importance. Placing the family at the centre of adoption does not mean the child's needs are being ignored. I am suggesting the opposite: if we take a wider, more person-centred view of adoption and all that goes into building a family, then the chances of adoption being successful – being a fulfilling, positive and lasting experience – for an even larger number of children and families will be increased. Our focus does not have to be only on the child and the child's immediate needs for those needs to be met.

As I have said before, adoption is dyadic: it has two parts, adopter and adoptee. The relationship that develops between the two is the golden thread at the very heart of adoption, and has to be painstakingly hand-woven over time. It can't be manufactured by a system or outsourced to professionals, although they undoubtedly can help through their compassionate understanding and patient support of families. Adoption policy and practice must change to better reflect the needs of both parents *and* children, and value them equally as they are brought together to create each new family unit. Family-making will require a significant shift in thinking, behaviour and attitudes, and major changes to the process of assessing and matching parents and children.

There is plenty of evidence-based knowledge about childhood trauma, attachment and the best ways of re-parenting traumatised children. This has been built up over many years from the fields of neuroscience, psychology and child development. There is substantially less knowledge about adoptive parents, what characteristics influence their relationships with their children and the impact of adoption on them.

Currently, the prime objective in assessing applicants is to establish whether or not they have the resources and skillset to provide permanence to a child. Emphasis is on ensuring they can meet the requirements that being placed with a child will bring. These preconditions are all about the child and are essentially Maslowesque: the child needs a caring home and all the material stuff that brings, a sense of security, relationship, love and so on. The assessment is concerned with what the adopter can provide; any vulnerabilities they may have are viewed from the likely impact this could have on a child, not what impact the child could have on them. Other than an investigation of their motivation to adopt, the applicants are not assessed on *their* needs or if any of their needs will be met. They undergo no psychological assessment.

If we continue to take the stance that adopters are a resource whereby a child can be provided with permanence, we will probably be stuck with this model. If we accept that, when individuals first come to adoption, they present as vulnerable people trying to make a life-changing decision and their needs are integral to the success of any future child-parent relationship, then matters change. Prospective parents need space, time, support and information to thoroughly work out if making a family this way will actually meet their needs and if they are prepared for the risks and differences that exist in this route to parenthood. They need help to carefully evaluate whether adoption is right for them. This cannot be speeded through and needs to be completed in a much more diligent way than currently. It must be the first priority, and driven by the prospective adopters. The requirements of the Prospective Adopters Report (PAR) come later, although some of that information may indeed be a natural consequence of those earlier discussions.

Some would say this already happens during the work done for the PAR, if the social worker is experienced and empathic. However, I am talking about using a significantly different mindset that sees the parent's needs as a prime consideration and focuses on what adoption could mean to them, not necessarily the child. This approach needs to have nothing to do with permanence and market economies; it must hide nothing and consider all the facts, with no positive spin. It should be guided by an independent mentor – not an assessor – who might be an experienced therapist, social worker or adoptive parent, or have input from all three.

Once prospective parents are approved, matching them with children must use a similar level of diligence and sophistication. Careful, informed, joined-up assessment and matching are essential to creating the golden threads of robust, lifelong family relationships. It cannot be rushed or driven by commercial considerations and the needs of *all* the participants have to be fully understood and taken into account. This may mean prospective adopters may need to follow different pathways, based on their motivation and needs. It will also require us to acknowledge the harsh truth that a minority of children find what we regard as 'normal' family life impossible. For them, the emotional demands that go with family relationships are literally unbearable, or impossible to meet; they are stuck, reliving their past and recreating the dysfunctional, stressful relationships they have always known. I suggest these children would benefit more from living in a therapeutic community where they are not expected to meet the concentrated emotional demands of family life and where intensive, professional multidisciplinary support, similar to that we finally obtained, too late, for Jemma, is available on a daily basis.

A far more thorough assessment of the needs of prospective adoptive parents, the likely impact that certain behaviours could have on them and their weaknesses as well as their strengths could help children's social workers and matching panels. A transparent and realistic approach to assessing both the needs and the challenges of the child must also be incorporated into this process. Regrettably, social workers often seem reluctant to spell out or even recognise the damaging aspects of a child's history from conception until placement. Sometimes essential information has been lost, sometimes its relevance is misunderstood; sometimes there is a misplaced reluctance by social workers to share it, on the grounds that it might colour adopters' attitudes and behaviour towards the child. A third of respondents in the 2017 BBC *File on Four* survey said they hadn't been given 'full and correct' information about their child pre-adoption.

The Selwyn report highlighted several key risk factors that should be considered when considering a child's ability to forge relationships and integrate into 'normal' family life. These include age at placement, the level and types of abuse the child suffered, the number of moves and length of time in the care system and the quality of their foster care. There are other well-known factors that affect a child's likely development, such as maternal exposure to violence (Levendosky, Bogat & Huth-Bocks, 2011) and drugs and alcohol (Mukhergee, Hollins & Curts, 2012). In my experience, some of these are often skated over in Child Permanence Reports – the most notable probably being whether the mother used drugs and alcohol during pregnancy, and the risk and implications of foetal alcohol syndrome. It is crucial that we improve the information provided and that matching panels understand exactly how the specific needs of both parties will be met when they bring children and parents together.

It is no good approving someone to adopt with reservations about the level of difficulty they can cope with and then matching them with two children whose backgrounds suggests they might present considerable challenges. It might work out but it might destroy them, at which point it will be construed as being due to their shortcomings, not those of the system. I have seen this happen numerous times. This is not a moral or effective way to achieve permanence and is certainly no way to treat people who have come forward in good faith and hope. All adoptive parents need to be provided with a full history, a fully researched and truthful trauma timeline for the particular child that may be placed with them, not a generic overview, and information on how it could affect the child now and for the rest of their life.

This informed approach is doubly important because it also provides a window on what needs the family are likely to have in the future. This, in turn, is critical because, if we want to help build new families, we also need to address the way we provide them with ongoing support.

Even though prospective adoptive parents are told that adoption is a lifelong commitment from day one, the system actually takes a far more short-term approach. Up until relatively recently, local authorities were only too happy to make a sharp getaway once the adoption order was granted. Almost all their funding and resources went into recruiting families and placing children with them; then, having completed the statutory checks, the families were left to get on with it.

This began to change around the time of the introduction of the Adoption Support Services Regulations 2005, and now more effort is put into post-adoption support, either directly or through other agencies. Prior to this, a small number of progressive voluntary agencies had identified the clear need and benefit of post-adoption support and were offering it, but it was not generally provided by local authorities. The practice has since continued to grow, but slowly, and there is still this emphasis on placing children rather than on developing and maintaining the golden thread of the parental relationship running through a child's life.

Many of the children placed in adoptive families have long-term, complex needs associated with their history, development or genetics. Usually these needs are only scantly addressed in any Adoption Support Plan. The funding for any support needs that *are* identified cannot be relied upon, even though the Adoption Support Fund (ASF) was set up to specifically address that issue. The ASF and the limits that have been imposed on how much each family can claim are covered in Chapter 8. Access to the fund is via a social work assessment and subject to approval by a management company that administers the fund, and this is not always straightforward. Some parents are finding it hard to get professionals to understand the level of difficulty they are experiencing with their children. I have spoken with families in crisis who have waited nine months and still do not know if or when that help might come.

Another dimension of the ASF, and adoption support in general, is that it is targeted purely at the needs of the child. The needs of parents, even where those needs are a direct result of their adoption experience, are not catered for. Interventions that directly help the parents are not seen as an ASF funding priority if they do not have any measurable impact on the child. In fact, adoptive parents are entitled to no direct adoption support for themselves. If their relationships, mental health, employment, living conditions or any other aspect of daily living become affected by the problems of caring for a severely traumatised child, it is regarded as their responsibility to deal with it; they are entitled to no specialised support in the way that adoptees and birth families are. Adoption is a lifelong issue in which parents and children both need support in addressing the inevitable and unique problems that arise from trying to build lasting families this way.

If we continue to concentrate on family-finding and permanence, ignore the needs of parents and fail to provide timely, adequate, effective support for *all* family members, then adoptions will continue to break down. If we choose to value and support both sides of the adoption dyad in a family-making model, then such breakdowns will become less likely. This requires the removal of the uncertainty that still exists around provision of that support, and it has to be fully funded and available as part of any adoption plan from the very outset.

The lifelong nature of adoption must also be acknowledged in how we research and develop adoption policy. Up until now this has not happened. The short-term approach is inevitable, given that this is a political issue; general elections are five years apart and so new initiatives come out every few years, while national and local budgets and contracts tend to be set and renewed annually, or every two or three years. As a result, adoption policy has developed in a piecemeal way, often with new bits being bolted on every few years to deal with some crisis or new need.

We only have to look back a few years to see how this plays out in practice and adds little value to the plight of adoptive families. In January 2013, the DfE issued *Further Action on Adoption: finding more loving homes* (DfE, 2013b), which built on work arising from *An Action Plan for Adoption: tackling delay*, (DfE, 2011), set out the next steps to be taken in tackling delay in placing children and identified the 'one outstanding challenge to the adoption system – finding enough adoptive parents'. Further initiatives followed, including the establishment of the Adoption Leadership Board in 2014 and a paper on regionalising adoption (DfE, 2015).

Then, as I've described earlier, in Chapter 4, in March 2016, the Secretary of State for Education unveiled a new blueprint for adoption, *Adoption: a vision for change* (DfE, 2016), building on some of the points raised in 2012 and 2013. This introduced a new four-year strategy that, according to the accompanying press release, had the aim to speed up adoption at its centre. By amending 'criteria used by social workers and courts', this strategy would 'tackle head on and overturn the damaging fall in adoption decisions which are letting vulnerable children down'. There were some other points in the plan that adoptive parents would have been pleased about, but these were focused on specific needs of the child, such as measures to boost their educational outcomes.

It is well known that the longer children are in care, the poorer their outcomes, and so speed can be important, but this focus ignores other factors. The press release accompanying the launch also talked about providing vulnerable children with support and stability, but it said nothing about golden threads and long-term outcomes or valuing adoptive parents. The blueprint's focus was still very much on the here and now and the short-term goal of getting children placed for adoption.

The 2013 Care Inquiry report told us that 'relationships must be the lens through which policy development should be tested, refined and reviewed' and that, hopefully, these relationships would last 'beyond childhood and into adulthood'. So, where is the 'lifelong' policy approach to adoption, and by this I mean a cohesive and fully funded 20–30-year strategy, informed by comprehensive and accurate data, including data on long-term outcomes (which, as I've previously observed, are significantly missing)?

Admittedly, long-term breakdowns are not always clear-cut separations and easily measurable. The 2013 Care Inquiry report talks about 'measuring *less tangible* outcomes about children's wellbeing' (my italics), and there may be several qualitative and subjective measures of whether an adoption has in fact broken down. These must primarily take into account the view of the child and the parent. In some instances, the view of professionals could also form a point of reference, especially where the dynamics are intractable, but caution needs to be applied here as I know of several adoptions where the professional view and the parent's view were in very sharp contrast. In these circumstances, the professional view normally prevails, and I question the validity of this in some cases.

These outcomes, regardless of how they are ultimately named or defined, must be accurately recorded as they are essential evidence of success rates and provide vital information to parents and professionals about the factors that can lead to disruption and breakdown. Without them it is impossible to evaluate anything fully, obtain a meaningful picture of what is going on in the world of adoption, or learn from mistakes. Good policy and practice can only be formulated if they are based on complete, accurate, truthful and relevant information.

We also need clarity regarding what any future research is actually about, because adoption and the adoption system are two different things and in the past have often been mistaken for each other. The Adoption Research Initiative, commissioned by the Department for Education and Skills, ran for about 10 years from 2002 and led to 11 reports from seven studies. Many were not about adoption per se but about the adoption system and practice. Some were about foster care and special guardianship. One study was dedicated to deciding whether the fee adoption agencies are paid is fair. We need a proper research programme into family-making, with the emphasis on adoptive *families* and *relationships* and the factors that influence them, from their perspective, not just those of the professionals and policy-makers.

Perhaps one of the biggest hurdles we face in moving to a family-making model is that of changing the attitudes I have described throughout this book. These are largely cultural and systemic, and each new generation of professionals and policy-makers is influenced by them. They promote assumptions about children, permanence and adoption, such as that parents are to blame if things go wrong and adoption is only about the child. Unfortunately, this dogma prevents creativity. It will take energy and perseverance to convince those in charge that there can be a better way to care for looked-after children that still meets targets. There are some simple things that we can do to help this process along. The language used, for instance, has a wide-ranging influence on how attitudes are formed and maintained.

I have read numerous reports, articles and books about adoption. I've noticed how rarely people who adopt are mentioned, even if the report has adoption as its title and focus. Many terms are still commonly used to describe a child's parents of birth (biological parent, real parent, natural parent, parent, mother, father) and for those who foster (foster carer, foster parent, foster mum, foster dad), but the term most generally used for those who adopt is 'adopter'. Sometimes 'adoptive parent' is used and, up until placement, 'prospective adopter'. But you commonly come across a list referring to 'children, birth parents, foster parents and adopters'.

Why and where did the term 'adopter' originate? It is, at least, better than 'substitute parent', which was used on the application form that Anne and I completed when we applied to adopt all those years ago, but you rarely see references to 'fosterers' in the literature, and certainly not 'birthers'.

I am making a serious point. The name by which I am known is a reflection of the status, respect and value with which I am held and how I am perceived. Ensuring that I am ascribed the title of parent, or father, or dad speaks volumes about my role within my family. It also says something vital to my children. It tells them that they are living with their parents, the people who are their forever family, and who care for them and love them above all others. It says a lot about our *relationship*.

Language influences attitudes. The 2013 Care Inquiry reported that people providing long-term, permanent foster care wanted to be called 'foster parents', as this would acknowledge the importance of those relationships within the family. Similarly, as you read this book, did you change your view of me and my role as Jemma's dad? And might that be because I started replacing the term 'adopter' with 'parent' over the last few chapters? Did you notice this?

Rethinking the language of adoption could help change attitudes and enable everyone to think differently about the role of adoptive parents and parenthood, moving away from seeing us simply as a route to permanency for a child to regarding us as their parents. This would also reinforce our children's sense of belonging and being part of a family, and hence their sense of permanency. This needs to start at the top, at government and policy-making level.

I have often felt invisible as an adoptive parent. We are, as I've said, part of the shadow side of adoption, often ignored, inconvenient and misunderstood. There is actually nothing to fear from shining light on us and much to gain but, unfortunately, we have been hidden from sight by all sorts of agendas and attitudes. No one wants to open that can of worms.

Like countless families, our adoption of Jemma has been long, arduous, traumatic. It did not match the life promises any of us would have hoped for, but here we are. Her needs were paramount but my life, my place in hers and my parenthood are equally important. Our adoption was not, and is not, about permanence or easing fiscal budgets. And social work is not central to it. It is about our relationships and how *we* became a family.

Both society and the state have a moral obligation to adoptive parents and the vulnerable and damaged children we grow to love. We can devise a better model of adoption, one that has fewer risks and takes account of the needs of the whole family. We may have to change the system and challenge the status quo, but surely it is in all our interests to do just that? Given the emotional and financial costs of disrupted adoptions, what more have we to lose?

References

Boddy J (2013). *Understanding Permanence for Looked-After Children: a review of research for the Care Inquiry.* [Online.] The Care Inquiry. www. nuffieldfoundation.org/sites/default/files/files/Understanding%20 Permanence%20for%20LAC.pdf (accessed 27 April 2018).

Care Inquiry (2013). *Making not Breaking: building relationships for our most vulnerable children.* [Online.] The Care Inquiry. https:// thecareinquiry.files.wordpress.com/2013/04/care-inquiry-full-report-april-2013.pdf (accessed 27 April 2018).

Department for Education (2011). *An Action Plan for Adoption: tackling delay.* London: Department for Education.

Department for Education (2013a). *Improving Permanence for Looked-After Children.* London: Department for Education.

Department for Education (2013b). *Further Action on Adoption: finding more loving homes*. London: Department for Education.

Department for Education (2015). *Regionalising Adoption*. London: Department for Education.

Department for Education (2016). *Adoption: a vision for change*. London: Department for Education.

File on Four (2017). *Adoption: families in crisis*. BBC Radio 4. www.listenersguide.org.uk/bbc/episode/?p=b006th08&e=b095rs05 (accessed 26 April 2018).

Levendosky A, Bogat GA, Huth-Bocks AC (2011). The influence of domestic violence on the development of the attachment relationship between mother and young child. *Psychoanalytic Psychology 28*(4): 512–527.

Mukhergee RA, Hollins S, Curts L (2012). Fetal alcohol spectrum disorders: is it something we should be more aware of? *The Journal of the Royal College of Physicians of Edinburgh 42*(2): 143–150.

Safe with Self-Injury:
a practical guide to understanding,
responding and harm-reduction

by Kay Inckle
(PCCS Books, 2017)

www.pccs-books.co.uk

Safe with Self-Injury is an essential resource for anyone who has a supporting role or relationship with someone who hurts themself. It is equally useful for people who self-injure, to help them to explore their experiences and to keep themselves safe. Based on interviews with people who self-injure and frontline practitioners who work with them, it explores why people hurt themselves, debunks myths and misconceptions, and explains self-injury in the contexts of human embodiment and a social model approach to distress. It provides practical strategies for responding helpfully, including a harm-reduction approach, and additional resources for policy writing.

'… an excellent contemporary account of self-injury and approaches to supporting people who self-injure. The book will be an invaluable resource for anyone working in the field.'
Hilary Lindsay, Director, Self-injury Support, Bristol

'This is an immensely useful text that carefully combines sociological insights with practical advice on responding well to self-injury… Grounded in principles of social justice, this is a thoroughly refreshing guide that will be of use to anyone who encounters self-injury in their personal or professional lives.'
Dr Amy Chandler, Chancellor's Fellow in Health, University of Edinburgh